RUTH'S
SKIRTS

In Memory
Bud Topping
Honey

each blade of grass
horse hair   russet potato
each salty daring ocean wave
and Halloween
the way the body works land

now I know these things
are peace
these things are justice

October, 2006

RUTH'S SKIRTS

KATHY ENGEL

IKON
New York, New York

Work in this collection has appeared in the following:
Poetry East, And Not Surrender: American Poets on Lebanon (an anthology); Street Magazine; WIN Magazine; Affilia; Nuestra Prensa; The East Hampton Star; Palestine Focus; New Directions for Women; Racing and (E)Racing Language: Living with the Color of Our Words (an anthology); Portside (online publication); Hut (online publication)

Cover art *Le Petit Déjeuner*, painting by Michael Aram,
  used by permission of Gaby de Gail

Cover and book design by Linda Gates,
  Gates Sisters Studio

ISBN: 0-945368-13-5
       978-0-945368-13-7

Library of Congress Control Number: 2007920253
First Edition
Printed in Canada by AGMV Marquis

This publication is made possible with
public funds from the New York State Council
on the Arts, a State Agency.
NYSCA

IKON
151 First Avenue, #46
New York, NY 10003
ikoninc@aol.com

RUTH'S SKIRTS

To The Reader	11
A Little Leopard	17

1. A Woman Inventing Heat

The Wreath	21
Salud, Helen	22
For The Strong Woman	24
An Arm For Haiti	26
Today	27
The Kitchen	28
For Ingrid	30
A Letter to my Soul	33
Now	36
Nora's Song	38
Serenade to Susan	40
The Day I Met Blanche	43
No Apathy Here	45

2. Home

Home	48
Daily Instruction To My Self	49
Good Fortune	51
Summer Morning: Second Life	52
Where The Lights Are	53
April Morning/Jaja	55
The Women in my Family #2	56
The Horses	57
Father's Day	58
Palestine Journal: Iron Hearts	59

3. Not a Protest Poem/ A Love Song

In The Middle of the Night in July   66
Negotiations   68
For Haiti   69
Not a Protest Poem/ A Love Song   71
Letter to the Editor   72
Bill   74
When the Killing of a Stranger Means the World 77
Chip Chip Chip   78
Just Another Day   80
Ambition   82
Prelude   84
Here's Why   86

4. Will I Have The Courage?   87

5. Conversation Between Heaven and Earth

Conversation Between Heaven and Earth   101
Prayer   105
Second Letter to my Mother   107
Spring/Inheritance   108
Prayer 2   110
What Matters: Honoring Betty Shabazz   112
Ruth's Skirts   116

About the Author   125

... it is a tremendous responsibility — a responsibility and an honor — to be a cultural worker... whatever you call this vocation. One's got to see what the welfare children see, what the scholar sees, to see what the ruling class mythmakers see as well, in order to tell the truth and not get trapped...

toni cade bambara
Voices of the Dream: African American Women Speak

For Ella and Jaja

To the Reader

THESE POEMS AND PROSE WRITINGS SPAN more than twenty five years.
I haven't placed them in chronological order because I think the
progression of life is a complex and surprising continuum that
doesn't reveal itself in a line-up of years. I have dated them to give
a sense of story and time. The writings have accumulated while I've
been organizing, producing, consulting — agitating — putting my
public work before my writing.

The writer Louise Erdrich said to me when we were at the
Macdowell Colony, in our twenties, that she thought my writing is
my attempt to "make things whole." I think she was right then and
now, about my politics and my writing — my life. And I've learned
that the poem is the action and the action is the poem. At times
my poem is MADRE or Stand with Sisters for Economic Dignity,
Women in Prison, Haiti. At times my public action is my writing or
performance. They flood together in one life even if they fight for
time, space. The writer craves silence and solitude. The activist seeks
community, public space, gets excited seeing a picket line. Just like
the organs of a body, they work together to make the whole.

Finally, it is the story that prevails.

I could not write a poem without my complicated, necessary,
beloved community. And I could not organize a campaign, write a
press release or imagine a project without poetry. I argue with the
barriers or artificial constructs that limit our abilities to imagine.
We need to conjure up all of our selves and unconscious powers
we're not even tuned into, so we can believe the change we know
is necessary, to fight the poverty of imagination that holds on to
poverty, and to domination. That requires not only the risk of
showing up, standing up or speaking up, but the risk of letting go,
the discomfort of the new, different, awkward.

I used to say the only thing I do completely by myself is write my poems. Now I have come to understand that even that I don't do alone. Each poem is the birth and life of relationships, community, the give and take between the people in my life and me. For that — those people — I am utterly grateful and enriched.

Thank You

Ella and Jaja for filling my life with meaning and joy in a way I couldn't even begin to describe. For surprising me, teaching me, inspiring me. Making each day possible, meaningful, hopeful...

Tinka, my mother, for always supporting me, believing in me in amazing ways regardless of what it is or whether it makes sense to you, for showing me that when something needs to be built — a school, an organization — you don't wait for anyone else; you do it.

Herman, my father for showing me about making art as resistance and change, that risking action is always better. For marching before me and with me. For reading me the first poems.

Jon, for a life together, our children. For giving back art to so many children. Growing things, building things, caring about beauty. For listening to the terrible first drafts before coffee or tea, and knowing what needs to go.

My sisters Susan and Jenno for loyalty, laughter, wisdom, generosity, secrets and brilliance. For intelligent, loving listening. All those walks. To Jake, Will, Sam, Maddie, Charlie, enriching me always and giving me hope.

My brother Tim for being there, tenacity, believing in me, for loving literature. For Jasper, Gavin, Ruby.

Sonya for showing me early what it is to be a strong, independent woman, fully engaged.

Huge, deep immeasurable thanks to Susan Sherman and Linda Gates for making this book happen, believing in it and me, helping me at every step in substantive, incredible ways, time, insight, true generosity. There's no way to thank you enough.

Alexis De Veaux, best friend, sister, for showing me what a poet life can be, breaking boundaries.

To Sonia Sanchez, mentor, sister, friend, always there, paving the way. Edwidge Danticat for thoughtful grace.

I speak to another world, sending love to my sister, the beautiful poet Safiya Henderson Holmes. Love to her daughter Naimah Henderson Holmes, her children Daljeem, Heaven, Zen.

Thanks to Diane Greene Lent for documenting beautifully, generously, for offering photos.

To Roger Haile for offering Chris's work.

Kickass Artists, friends, colleagues, path cutters who've taught me, stood by me, put up with me, helped me... Gwendolen Hardwick, Tiye Giraud, Gale P. Jackson, Suheir Hammad, Valerie Maynard, Danny Glover, Patrice Gaines, Sandra Betancourt Garcia, Clare Coss, Leslie Cagan, Jessica Leighton, Margaret Ratner, Kica Matos, Blanche Wiesen Cook, Melanie Kaye/Kantrowitz, Maria Hinojosa, German Perez, Digna Sanchez, Susan L. Taylor, Rosalba Rolon, Alvan Colon Lespier, Susan Sarandon, Annie Hess, Phyllis Bennis, Rev. Osagyefo Uhuru Sekou, Marsha Norman, Belvie Rooks, Rony & Cathryn Shimony, Tamar Cole, Laura Flanders, Harriet, Toby and Allison Barlow, Dan Steiger, Caron Atlas, Marie Brown, Carole Alexis, Vivian Stromberg, Jean Jean-Pierre, Mahdis Keshavarz, Billie Jean Young, Anasa Troutman, David Lerner, Tamar Kraft-Stolar, Myrna Cunningham, Joanne Biaggi, Lana Budheiri, Yasmin Adib, Eve Ensler, Anasa Troutman, Grace Paley, Zala Chandler, Fitzgerald Taylor, Brenda Levin, Judy Arthur, Virginia Giordano... The too many to name sisters and brothers and organizations who have led the ways for me, in this journey of poetry, love and movement work — I hope you know who you are; I wish I could name you all; I thank you.

Jesse Pasca for technical assistance in the nick of time!

In memory: my grandmothers, each: Henrietta Engel, Lina P. Derecktor. My aunt Rosa, who has courage.

Thanks to Eileen Hoffman, Christina Lindstrom for health.

Teachers Jane Cooper, Jean Valentine, Galway Kinnell.

June Jordan in memoriam.

In memory: Ingrid Washinawatok, Donald Walter Woods, Nora Astorga, Sandy Pollack, Damu Smith, Bill Kunstler...

The late Director of the Academy of American Poets, Elizabeth Kray

Ussachevsky who showed me creative leadership, gave herself to poetry.

Special thanks to Sonya Friedman and Herman Engel for the book cover, and to Gaby de Gail for permission.

Thanks to the Blue Mountain Center and The Macdowell Colony where early poems were written.

MADRE, United For Peace & Justice, The Center For Constitutional Rights, Stand With Sisters For Economic Dignity, Gates Sisters Studio, Women in Prison Project, Hayground School...

Kathy Engel
Sagaponack, NY
2006

A Little Leopard

In another era (or another place)
We would be called   *old*

My sister says
After a certain age   *women shouldn't*

Someone told my friend
Gorgeous shekere   music   streaming gold and red
Glitter in her skin, eyes
Hair of many worlds   someone told her:

After 40 no leopard and tiger stripes!

I say
A little leopard
Sometimes
Can be a good thing

Then shorten my skirt

She says
That's a poem!
We walk down the street
Singing Langston:
Life is fine!
Life is fine!

2004 for Tiye

1.

A Woman Inventing Heat

The Wreath

for Muriel Rukeyser

Because it hangs on the door
Because the door opens
and anyone can enter
Because it is the color of the sun singing
through the cells of the earth
Because it is an open circle
through which our prayers can breathe
Because it has fine tiny spears
from the arms of the tree
Because we long for something whole
that will not tear away from us
Because in a circle we find
justice
the folding over of the dead and the living
Because in a circle we find
magic

Because it is a ring
like the ones creased in years on the tree trunk
or shining red yellow around the wound
illuminating it

Because it is a gathering together
of many bodies: nutty bell-shaped pine cones
gentle pierce of needles
burst of spruce
and cranberries scattered like small red balls of light

Because it is a promise

1980

Salud, Helen

For years before we met
I heard your name singing out

through the bodies of women
wombs usurped

tongues entangled
by the language of force

you walked in light on this earth
illuminating

a humility
hard to fathom

daily work and the colors of compassion
woven like the glorious orange, purple, green

shawl I imagine you wearing
in a warm evening breeze

at the end of a conference day
somewhere in the world

where women and men gather
to name possibility

café de Caribe
fragrant earth sip

skin glow, mother island
fruit   sun   *poesia*

finest grains of sand
trespassed

each battle ground
a place of beauty

a woman's body
an island, a scar

every gracious door opening
a chance to engage

what is health?
salud

you, dear Helen, querida compañera, doctora, hermana,
you were health, you are

2002

Dr. Helen Rodriguez-Trias
July 7, 1929 — December 27, 2001

For the Strong Woman!

No anorexic thigh-less triangle-spaced —
my legs have character
substance

give pumps a new meaning
they could take you places
I should rent them out:
tired of those skinny ankles,
sleek slim thighs?
Call me...

I no longer apologize
for my legs
I don't say:
Honey don't you wish I made nylons sing?
That seam up the back of sheer black pantyhose
talks back on my legs.

I've formed a new organization
Legs With A Purpose.
Cyrano could have enjoyed
such an affiliation
had he realized
he wasn't alone.

These legs could distinguish me.
They're independent
willful.
I read about a woman who stopped pasta and seltzer
to change her thighs.
I want to tell her:

Sweetie: maybe your thighs were telling you something.

My legs will wrap around you,
squeeze you like a cobra
if you're not careful,

won't stand for
cat calls
or racist slurs.
My legs are spurs.

They're ample homes.
No cold bony rejectionist legs.
No puritanical thighs.
There's room for you there.

My legs have history,
culture.
You can't hold legends
On a wire.

Leggings legs,
I need to move freely.
No Chanel gambs here.

These legs are revolutionary,
disciplined.
I listen to my legs.
They're a political party
and they aim to win.

1990's

An Arm For Haiti

for Alerte

from just beyond the elbow
an arm   one human arm
one female arm
imagine the fingers
imagine their work
the detail of their daily travel
imagine the palm
soft imprint
the cushion
telltale lines
leading somewhere
imagine the wrist
did it wear a watch
how did the bones fit
so delicate

she could not bury her arm
she could not nurse her back
and neck
she could not say goodbye
when she was left to die

imagine
a woman in her home
she lifts her arm to protect her face
she lifts her arm in the air

1992

Today

for Louise Erdrich

In the Black Hills FBI agents hunt Indians.
Deer leap to safety here in Mondadnock.
Young men sign up for a license to kill.
The sun sets regardless,
a last splash releasing the room from its walls.

At the wooden table, coffee mugs wrapped in our hands,
Louise and I meet in transit. We're tending
someone's house, wipe up every crumb, sponge off the spills
and breathe into photographs, say the names aloud.
At ten my best friend and I pricked our fingers,

pressed the tips together and traded blood.
Here with my new friend
we lie down each alone in separate rooms to dream.
Our unfilled curves fill the air.
We drink pots of coffee, build a fire

that will sputter and wheeze with maple, birch
and balled up newspaper until the house creaks with night.
Hiroshima, Nagasaki. The consonants slip
from our tongues like ice into water.
We've come to these woods to reconstruct.

Louise is Ojibway. With tapered fingers
she digs up her tribe's treaty, holds it
to light, measures dimensions. I take out
the t-square to get the angles right, saw off
chunks of wood and work at putting things back together.

We write letters home, pencil in our progress.
The trees move into their winter skins.
Grey limbs slice the sky; soon Louise will get on a bus.
The stars tell us we're circled by a common moon.
The trees won't leave. Something we build will last.

1980

The Kitchen

paintings and sculpture by German Perez

inside the red night
strands
hair and fire and water: tongues

freshly cut lemon spits
its baptism

each spice
a woman
inventing
heat

she measures
sifts
she whisks, slices

salt, water, corn
table, bed, window

phylo sheets of dough
thinly rolled

the hand
reaches inside the warm beginning

the hand
cracks

her hair
leads to a world outside this one
the sea sweeps in news
her language cuts the bread
he waits in his chair at the table for his food
locks the door with the hammer of his voice

several times a day
the gathering
each telling a late root pulled: turnip, parsnip, yam;
each telling a body organ: liver, kidney, heart

what taste
has not folded into her oiled palm?
what ocean has not rutted her cheek?
what bit of cloth has not soaked her blood and the blood of her food?
what herb has she not cupped in her hand and buried in the ground
   like ash,
some of its dust sticking in her throat,
a clutch of grief that won't rinse down,
a seed

what endures?

the pot on the wall
used
scoured
returned

she reaches for a rope
climbs towards the top of the house
she never makes it
the house opens
then closes

she becomes the greens she cuts
garlic she peels
oil of olive
drops of milk
earth colored nipples opening

her dream is a window

one arm irons

the other cradles
the infant curved in the arc of her torso, a second skin
mouth to breast
breast to sky

madre, abuela, tia, hermana

2001

For Ingrid

(Excerpt)

There I was, driving through the Wisconsin expanse Ingrid loved so. Ice fishing. Snow. Endless fields. Clusters of white birch. Her mom and sister in their beauty. Her mom said they were overwhelmed by the people, understanding in a different way now what Ingrid did, the places she traveled, the people with whom she worked, the risks she took, her wide reach, boldness.

Menominee. Ingrid's home. We were there. At the Res. Everything flowed together. The faces, the voices, the embraces, the tears, the silences and the words. The luminescence of Ingrid's eyes and smile in her velvet dress on the photo on the coffin. The plaques of recognition — "Indian of the Year," the Frederick Douglass Award, the Fannie Lou Hamer Award. The serving of the food. Her plate. Men drumming, dancing, stories. The offering of tobacco. The instructions. The nephews she adored. The one dancing, swooping down into his sorrow, shoulder to the floor, the depth of his pain pulling his torso to the earth. The tiny sounds escaping her son Maeh-ki as I held him. "This is my cousin," he introduced. The last instructions: her four day journey "home." Sending her out the window on her journey. The large window open for her, cool Wisconsin air flowing in. *Don't show your tears to the west; she might stop. Don't look back. Visit with the family while she travels. Ask her things; she's powerful in her journey.*

People I hadn't seen in years. People I had only heard of. People who didn't get along or had become estranged, now embraced. People from whom I had become estranged. "Ingrid brought so many people together," Billie Jean said, laughing and crying at once, squeezing me.

I prefer not to think someone has to die for that to happen. I prefer to think she offers a gift, a lesson, and the question is what we do with that gift. How we live and how we are sent off matters. Ingrid's gift was in acceptance, optimism, largesse. And humility. She didn't think she did anything unusual; just what she needed to do. With great enjoyment and *joie de vivre*, large sweeping movements of hand and arm, large voice, large embrace. In celebrating her and mourning her, people re-grouped like birds flying and flocking.

The acknowledgement of who she was, who we all are, our
fragilities and strengths, our vulnerabilities, shared commitments,
brought us close. All related. For a time. Underneath we grapple,
each in our own way, with the fury and injustice, the unknown,
unanswered. No one can make that okay. It doesn't go away. The
brutality. What do we do with it?

Carry on. Honor the earth, the water, the air — each other. Get a
little bigger. Honor our pain and struggle. Honor our quirks and
hers, don't memorialize into sainthood. Ingrid was real and funny
and quirky too. And while she brought us together these past days
and weeks and we held ourselves together, as Margo said she would
be mad right now. She would want to know the truth about what
happened. Demand to know.

Right and wrong isn't always so clear. But there are times when it
is deadly clear. Clear as the menstrual blood of women flooding
through history. Clear as fire. Clear as the trees, their bare limbs
leaning towards warmth. Outside my window a small red bud
pushes through a maple, through the wind and timeless day,
announcing itself.

On the Menominee Reservation I bought my daughters turquoise
rings like my mom got me every summer at Shinnecock as a child.
I've never bought myself a ring, but I chose a beautiful orange coral
set in silver.

Ingrid's husband Ali said the morning of the funeral that two
eagles had flown by and landed.

Ingrid guided my trip home. Sherry and Margo reminisced in
the car about the old days. The airline people didn't fuss when
I changed my flight. Where I doubted, Ingrid was always sure
things would work out. On the plane I told Margo I wanted her
AIM (American Indian Movement) t-shirt. She gave it to me.
Embarrassed, I started to give it back. "When an Indian gives
you something, never give it back," she admonished. I kept it;
we laughed. She had told me earlier in the week that Ingrid had
wanted us to be friends.

The trip was smooth. Then funny. From LaGuardia back home were a series of stops and waits and entertainment by Margo's five year old; everyone was helping each other to get where we needed to go. Margo's husband met us at the airport; Sherry's husband met us at Margo's. By the end of the night, in our exhaustion, we just laughed.

At 2:30 a.m. I opened my door. Ingrid's candle was lit. When I had told my seven-year-old that I was going to Wisconsin she cried and clung to me. "I don't want you to go." I knew it was real, the fear she felt because of what had happened to Ingrid and what it did to us. I told her I had to say goodbye to Ingrid. When I returned to find the green candle lit, I knew she had lit it.

I ate six day old pasta, bathed, got in bed and held Jon. I had felt silent all day, barely able to talk. Now I held life. Love. Then I cried.

I keep seeing Ingrid's wide open energetic face. Her sparkle. Everywhere I look I see her. How could anyone shoot her? How? That is the question we are all asking privately in our own minds again and again and again like a mantra. It's impossible to imagine the horror. What did she say? What did she go through? Ingrid could talk anyone into or out of almost anything.

Today my daughters took special things that Indian friends had given them and laid them on the table with the Guatemalan fabric, candle, flowers and Ingrid's photo we made as an altar.

Early this morning it snowed — a big burst of white fluffy winter blasting and billowing from the sky intercepting spring. Now, just before dusk, a shaft of light sings through the treetops, the sun opens into a soft glow. Ingrid's journey. Flying Eagle Woman.

1999

Internationally known indigenous human rights activist Ingrid Washinawatok, with two others, was kidnapped and murdered, apparently, by a rogue faction of the FARC-EP, Revolutionary Armed Forces of Colombia, when she was in Colombia, South America working to learn about and support the U'wa Indians. The U.S. government never fully investigated the case.

A Letter to my Soul

for Alexis

You gave me your raincoat.
I wore it like a sister
wrapped around me,
proud, announcing
its origin.

That's the way we wear
each other
right?
Loose or tight
we never let go.

You gave me a bureau
big and dark
full of drawers
for your goddaughter

it's yours baby
you said.

We filled it with dreams
wished it into life

a bureau with wings.

You gave me a ring,
is it okay, you asked
purple for love
silver for courage.

We are

two rivers
out of two sea-mouths
foreigners
from the same ancient sea.

We traveled to the war
together
came home warriors.

We traveled to peace
together
came home singing.

Looked up and found
too many soldiers dead
too many sisters gone.

I talk to your grandmother
sometimes, say her name
like a stream in the mountain.

Ruby Hill, I say,
we never spoke,
but I buried you too.

We're related,
remember?

This is a letter about friends.
It's raining
and I've got your coat.

I'm putting your goddaughter to bed,
we cross fingers,
build a new world.

As a child my Dad's Mom saved pennies
for a piano lesson
on the Lower East Side.
Mom's mom wore silk.

Ruby Hill
was a schoolteacher down South.
Jobless in New York,
she washed a white woman's sheets.

Could've been my grandma's
could've been...

The sheets on our beds
sting —

Africa to Palestine
Harlem to Tribeca
Buffalo to Bridgehampton.

We wash them,
lay down in hope.

I'm singing your goddaughter to sleep,
off-key,
determined to keep dreaming.

She asks about waterbeds, Buffalo, your house.

I show her a photo.
We bought our homes the same budding week.

You, poet, sweep all fifteen rooms
of your Buffalo dream house.

Whoever might clean for pay
could be someone's grandma.

I can't sew
like my mother
but thumb over thumb
we stake out a new stitch.

I'm reading your goddaughter to sleep
in her hew house
she tells me
your poem *Race &   Class&   Da Canine Experience*
laughing about the dog and the shit!

Are we crazy, outdated
to think of a life where poems
do feed

birds, at least,
cure disease, maybe?

I'm kissing your goddaughter goodnight
and tell her a story
about women
making something together.

This is what lasts
I tell her.
Ideals we work for.
Love makes it real.

1995

Now

for Safiya

1.

> *you sift*
> *the blue*
> *for the agate*

a line you dreamed
I wrote

each word
clay between us

in the conscious light of day
things are meant to make sense

we trade metaphor
no flash, no map

a flag of colors and language
startling the sky we draw with a pencil

an intractable
desire

for a truth
we wrap ourselves around.

2.

when your grandson
holds your face to his

sucks you into his one year marvel
you sift the blue for the agate

those years you healed with your hands
the branches of your fingers

diligent
each stroke a villanelle

when you poet
long limbed, sinuous

open eyed
exquisite in what you know

the blue for the agate
sifts through

the sifting is how we travel
alone, together

alone again

the agate
is what you see

the blue
is your truth

1998

Nora's Song

for Nora Astorga

You're skating
even in Managua
en la playa tambien
you're skating Nora
on ice through the U.N.
down Second Avenue
through the formal doors
of meeting rooms
into your youngest child's bedroom
on the runway of the Sandino Airport
even on the stretcher
with an oxygen mask
you are skating
negotiating on ice
writing speeches with your skate blades
eating mangoes with your mittens
breathing circles of frosty air
talking men and kids and sipping margaritas
dreaming it all
your eyes are skating dark on the shimmering ice
(this ice has never known such loving battle)
your shoulders are skating
your young woman mother's body is skating
full tilt
in a red dress
swinging
to Ghana
you are skating
home you are skating
yes home, Nora
in your heart
tu pais
tus compas
skating into home
a compassion beyond victory
and those who love you

everywhere
known and unknown
in towns and villages and cities and on back roads
find little ponds and indoor rinks and huge lakes
and even rivers that stand still for a moment
to skate
skate furiously
with you

1988

Nora Astorga was Nicaragua's Ambassador to the United Nations at the time of her death, due to cancer, on February 14, 1988, age 38. She had three wishes before dying: to return to Ghana, which she wasn't able to do, to take her children ice skating, which she did, and to return home to her beloved Nicaragua. She was able to go home for the last six weeks of her life.

Serenade to Susan

Hey Jersey girl, are
you now or have you ever
talked Nicaragua

been spied on, stood out
on some cold official steps,
the nation's capitol

for a wire story,
a headline we couldn't get,
beret tilted,

a strategic call
in the wind? Just when I think
you're about to get

cynical, a tear
fights down those famous cheeks.
At La Casa de

Las Madres in
Chinandga, Nicaragua,
Alexis suddenly

called out: *A Cinquente
Años Sandino Vivé!* Your
face melded with Rosa's face

as you swallowed
the Chinandega earth
in the hills far from any

reporter but
Atlantic City, the movie,
was playing in Managua.

Just when I think you'll cry,
a wry grin takes over,
you drop a quip, keep

us honest. Just when
you might say: *enough!* you stand
bolder, funnier.

Once you said:
Use me to be
effective. That's the point.

You and Tim took
the world's microphone
sparkling in your Oscar best

succinctly insisted
a red ribbon meant
Haitian refugees

incarcerated
at Guantanamo, meant a woman,
a name. You read aloud

Yolande Jean's letter
to her children in Haiti
in the CCR office

on Broadway
as she walked the HIV
wire, stopped eating.

That night in your evening gown
beside Tim
her words rushed through

you still,
holding you, a river
of mothers calling their children.

Last spring you strutted
through an uptown precinct
protesting police violence

in your tank top. Encircled
by admirers you
joked about telling reporters

what designer you
wore for the arrest.
Then you answered provocative

questions on TV
never missing a beat.
Mussolini made the

trains run on time
you said to Larry King
referring to the mayor.

We marvel at the
way you do your homework
how the words come out carved, clean
just tough enough.

So, we're here still.
Tonight we celebrate that
and your abundant

capacity for friendship,
your compassion and wit,
readiness and loyalty.

That's what brought us together
keeps us together.
Promise to

stay standing on your truths,
stay loud *and* soft,
funny *and* humble.

A toast to the good Catholic girl
playing waitress
and mom, nun and gunslinger

tossing diapers
salad
red hair

lusciously defiant.

The Center for Constitutional Rights (CCR)
Honors Susan Sarandon.
January, 2000

The Day I Met Blanche

for Blanche Wiesen Cook

It was "1908"
a warm day in November
not unlike today.
She was wearing cowboy boots,
a fluffy Jewish 'fro
crowned her animated face.
Clare was standing near
her silverblonde hair newly shorn,
a glint of wild outlaw.
We imagined voting,
met in an Italian restaurant
to celebrate
(always celebrate)
each other, our brilliance
and lament
(always lament)
the state of the world.
Jon was with us;
he sported a dashing Guatemalan vest,
schoolboy vigor.
Kathy! Blanche called out across the room —
You look fabulous!
What are we going to do?
How should I know? I laughed.
We have to organize! she proclaimed.
Take our country back.
We must speak to Crystal Eastman.
How do we build a movement? Clare mused.
We need to talk to Lillian Wald and her Women's Peace Party.
An emergency meeting.
I ordered pasta
Blanche wine
Clare sparkling water
Jon proposed a toast
to the brave women of the 20th century.
We went home
imagined Motown
and danced through the night

calling up
spirits of lives to come.
We could start...
the *women's international league for peace & freedom,*
we could march around the Pentagon,
burn our.... undershirts???...
Eleanor was still young.
We were waiting for our sisters to be born.
We were waiting for the new world.

It was 1908, November,
W.E.B. Du Bois
had identified
the problem of the 20th century.

It was 1908
and we were hopeful.

1994

In 1994 I asked Blanche Wiesen Cook for a recommendation for a fellowship, and (mistakenly) she began her letter..."In 1908 when I first met Kathy..."

No Apathy Here/ Happy Mother's Day!

Don't talk to me about apathy. Or young people's lack of involvement. Maybe you're standing in the wrong place. So look around and be proud; youth in America are on the move. I'm telling the truth; I traveled with nine of them Sunday April 25th, 2004 to what was called the largest protest in the history of the U.S., and saw zillions of them — all sizes, shapes, colors, languages and several genders!

They covered the nation's capitol with every kind of hair style and t-shirt, arm in arm with each other, and with moms, dads, grandparents, toddlers and octogenarian men wearing pink t shirts saying: This is What a Feminist Looks Like!

When I stumbled on two bodies curled up against the door in my daughter's room at 1:45 Sunday morning I knew I had entered a new era of my life! For weeks we had been trying to figure out whether we could manage spending the night in D.C., how many drivers we had, if we would take the bus and from where. I was nervous about the arrangements, and having to stay awake to drive the extra two hours to NYC and home again! Our numbers kept increasing; Long Island buses were full! After finally having to turn some kids down because the cars were full and the NYC buses were full; ten of us — eight young women and one young man ages twelve to nineteen — and I, left our home in Sagaponack at 2:30 a.m. Sunday morning April 25th to be part of history, to be counted for women's health rights, dignity and justice. Some of the young people had marched many times; and for some it was their first public protest experience — a twenty three hour wave.

My daughters and friends had gone a few weeks earlier to one of my favorite local haunts, Atlantic Coast Embroidery, to make their own t shirts with their own words: Get Your Laws Off My Body and It's My Choice. Amidst the dazzling array of feminist fashion (including stickers on nipples and huge paper mache vaginas), our home grown shirts actually attracted quite a bit of praise!

For me and people like me who have been wearing t shirts with messages and buttons that ruin your clothes and traveling at crazy hours to shout and sing and cry and finally hope, yesterday was a kind of reunion as well as a drop of glistening water in the long desert trek. Yes, hope! But the day also showed itself to be a new union. A wildly welcome, necessary, beautiful *new union*. I can't remember seeing so many young people all different, wonderful and energetic, at a political event. So many young men! And I kept running into daughters of my friends, with their groups. There were about sixty students just from one small upstate SUNY college.

The women's movement has evolved as a result of long, hard work, thought, struggle. The understanding of what *choice* means is now authentically inclusive of women from different class and ethnic backgrounds and throughout the world. The fuller definition of health and health rights invites broad ownership. Campuses are organized. The young participants exude a sense of power and certainty; they are where they are meant to be, in charge and speaking out.

Of our group some avidly documented with video cameras, some shouted and swayed, some watched; all appeared moved. When we heard that a television news commentator had called it the biggest demonstration in U.S. history I felt like the air lifted in the chests of these 9 people under the age of 20. Their faces even shifted a bit. One of the young women called home; her mother had seen her twice on television! They had experienced something they would never forget. And wanted to know what was next.

My friend the writer Alexis De Veaux said: *Being a mother is not simply the organic process of giving birth to a child; it's a way of being in the world.*

My kids were at the last big women's march twelve years ago, along with my mother. My younger daughter was in a stroller that day, and they have been to many different marches since.

Sunday April 25th, 2004, traveling with their friends as well, I felt another dimension of motherhood. And I share that sense with friends who've never given birth or raised children in their homes but are teachers and mentors and care givers. I feel so grateful for these young people, to be with them, for them to rub off on me. They are kind, intelligent and getting ready.

This April more than a million young and older and old humans from across these states stood up for women's lives and health and justice. Kate Clinton, the inimitable comedian, hosted the rally in D.C. and quoted Ché (Guevara) (*or was it Cher* she quipped!!) saying that the true revolutionary's greatest weapon is optimism. Maybe that's what we have going for us: weapons of mass optimism.

April 26, 2004 for Nuestra Prensa

2.

Home

Home

after Katrina

Olive tree still
calls the sky
from dry
ground
cayenne seas.
Women who work together
gave me green red tapestry
during war.
I placed it on my daughter's wall when she was three.

In that same ground of sacred old stories
where poem means *to aim*
an ageless man
skin creased gold
stood beside a sheet of plastic on a stick
one small table left intact.
He waved his arms in the bulldozed stubble air:
the children... they've been taken.

My new brother near what was bayou
told me
after the storm
in the shelters people fought to move their cots
closer to each other
what we know, what we have
is community
we will stay and fight for our space
fight for our space

let's get it out in the open
each name of pain
unaccounted for:
borderline, travesty, occupied
shanty, refugee, abandoned —

our work is to make language
hold the letters in every alphabet in our tongues

it's always about home
always about home

> *September, 2005*
> *Katrina*

48

Daily Instruction To My Self When the bombing is there, responsibility here (words when there are no words)

1. Upon waking, intercept thinking or feeling or opening eyes with breath

2. When allowing thought and feeling, let it be Ella and Jaja first, let it be the reminder of why, then a bird or something green/ growing, more children, more love filling your chest to stomp out the crawlers scratching in no language

3. Touch first

4. Take one baby aspirin for middle aged blood

5. Write at least one word in black notebook
before anything else, especially e-mail or newspaper

6. Read a new poem before same —
something unexpected

7. Drink coffee, dark, Arabic, fragrant beans, taste the twigs and soil like night in morning... never again think of giving up coffee.

8. Remember the Auschwitz survivor's words: *Don't be general.*

9. Read Mahmoud Darwish while drinking coffee and folding laundry and putting dishes away and sweeping and cutting flowers and folding and putting and cutting and sponging off little spots of...

10. Find air and put body in it

11. Run miles

12. Sweat miles

13. Remember exact words, faces, hand movements, intonation of those you met in West Bank, Jerusalem, Gaza, say them aloud and say a word in another language

14. Look at love like a two pound newborn in an incubator

Bandage it like a hummingbird's broken bones

Hold it — long hard-worked love — keeps growing back through tornado and tangled roots; turn to the person in an unexpected moment and tell him/her — a sigh, syllable or stroke

16. Now you may check e-mail, sign petitions, plan things

17. Be deliberate

18. Walk to the garden, pick vegetables, turn everything into ceasefire

19. Listen to Miles Davis, John Coltrane, Chucho Valdez, Mercedes Sosa, Nina Simone, while cooking

20. Take the clippers and basket and cut more flowers and put them everywhere

21. Do not nag children about stupid things

22. Do not stay angry about stupid things or take the wrong things personally

23. Cook beautiful meals for people you love

24. Make room for many teenagers to sleep all over the house, sprinkle poetry in corners

25. Be asymmetrical

26. Check on mother

27. Check on father

28. Attempt to see from within another

29. Say the dangerous truth and risk sounding rhetorical: "U.S. speeds up bomb delivery for the Israelis" NY Times" (July 22. 2006) — U.S. blocks call for immediate ceasefire at Rome meeting...

break the silence which is not a veil but a jail, a killing of soul and history, one life after another

30. CEASEFIRE

July 22, 2006

Good Fortune

for Dan

The peace sign on my road
was laid down after-hours
Robin Hood
a gardener
who resists pulling weeds
and his merry
young men
remind me all is not lost
their sweet faces and plentiful hair
some scruffy —
red paint on pavement
an arrow towards our house
Narrow Lane
is broad
and as a great preacher said
when we gathered
to honor our young
help is on the way

June 2003

Summer Morning: Second Life

for Jon

In our middle years
we rise early.

This day
having grieved

we once again
wake with hope:

you in your garden
tilling green

me in my nightgown
with new reading glasses

and last night's
poem.

I leave you notes,
permission to mourn.

You listen,
encourage — a haiku, perhaps.

Justine's asleep
with the story she wrote before bed:

Afraid of a Normal Corn Muffin.
Ella's visiting.

You cut the lettuce;
today we will live.

1999

Where the Lights Are

Something about the first snow. Why is that first falling and covering of crystal so breathtaking? Perhaps it's the quiet — branches heavy, blanketing of white powder.

The holiday lights seem to twinkle on trees earlier each year, magical, fairy tale like. Maybe the magic is that we've made it through another year; we can still fantasize, gather together, sip hot cocoa, run around with torn mittens and lips too cold to say words right.

Then there is the other side of it, that extravaganza of lights and front yard displays — whole lit up villages — reindeer and Santa's on lawns — a dimension of decoration I've never quite understood. I wonder particularly in these energy-fear days just how much electricity the flood of holiday lights takes.

This season I can't stop feeling something else about the lights as I drive by one beautifully lit tree after another, even as I sigh with a kind of relief that we can still enjoy the beauty, and perhaps an inner relief that I can return to warmth, light, home, that no matter where I've traveled, into what pain and danger, I've always so far been able to come home.

On September 12, 2005, soon after the storm swept through New Orleans and the Gulf Coast revealing the waves of neglect and disregard that cursed poor black communities long before; I went to Jackson, Mississippi and New Orleans with a friend in response to a call issued by the newly formed People's Hurricane Relief Fund & Oversight Coalition. The commitment of the PHRF was for self determination in all aspects of relief, recovery and reconstruction for the people hit the hardest, abandoned the longest.

We arrived in Jackson, Mississippi one hour after the Coalition leaders began to set up their office. We stayed with young organizers and educators from the Young People's Project, children of the Civil Rights Movement, who dazzled us with their talent, commitment, warmth and strength. These young people are paving the way for democracy, or at least for some truth at a time when denial has blinded the collective vision and eroded the soul of a big piece of this country.

One of the days we visited The Common Ground Collective in Algiers just across the river from New Orleans where white vigilantes had terrorized the black community in the wake of Katrina's winds. The Red Cross hadn't come. FEMA hadn't come. Humvees and Blackwater security personnel cruised the streets.

The police had looked the other way when white men randomly shot black men, graffiti sprawled across doors: *We Shoot Looters.*

The looters turned out to be every government agency. The people getting shot had been written off long ago.

Weeks ago, when the first lights began to flicker on again in New Orleans, the city became a patchwork of electricity. Some neighborhoods had lights; others, even nearby, remained dark. Since hearing this I have been haunted by the simple, harsh truth — the exact visual image of where the lights did or didn't go back on. I've been trying to think of what could be done during this holiday season, with lights, to show solidarity with the people who were left to die by the officials, to say: *lights for all or lights for none.* I don't know, in the magnitude of pain and need, whether a symbolic action of turning lights off for five minutes and then on again on New Year's Eve, or another particular day or many days, would mean anything.

What I do know is that we as a vast country of people have the capacity for great compassion and generosity. That has been proven. The question I ask is do we have the will to look at the truth and act on it? My New Year's challenge for this America, specifically the white part of America, is to insist that we look deep into the skin of our history, into our own mirrors, and ask ourselves what we can do to make sure there are never never any more broken levies, no more stranded people of any color, that safety is never preserved only for those who can pay for it, that we insist upon change, and that we seek out, as one of the leaders of the coalition has said so often " the hidden genius in each poor black community" and shine the lights on that genius. Shine the lights.

December, 2005

Published in the East Hampton Star, Dec. 2005, and online Portside and Hut-Articles

April Morning/Jaja

1.

This morning Jaja and I walked
before school
or even breakfast
down the road towards Steve Miller the artist
and the railroad tracks
past the farm workers camp
now forcibly vacated
across from the neighbor with a tree nursery,
two tall sons
and a blue door

Jaja was barefoot in the cold April early air
red flannel Christmas pajamas
and a yellow jacket
long hair flowing
I had my coffee cup in hand
could barely keep from
kissing her too much
the pure beauty of her eight year intention

2.

Jaja writes a poem every night.
She says a line
holds her pen up in the air
then muses: *No that's not right*
changes a word
changes it again:
Lift, not *carry. Raise* not *lift!*

When it *is* right
she underlines
with a flourish
closes the notebook
smiles.

2000

The Women in My Family #2

for Sooz and Tink

Ten years later
we traipse through my sister's kitchen
blue and white coffee mugs
still in our hands
this time our breasts leak with life
three generations full
milk shooting in an arc
onto our breakfast, each other,
lifetimes of sisters and mothers and daughters
passing at 3 am
naked in the night
rocking and walking and cooing
the future bundled on our shoulders
cat skimming the screen door and
the late movie left on with no sound
remember this:
the sisters' infants
breathed the same first spring
and the same first warm glow
sunk into their palm sized buttocks
as they lay on a quilt on the grass
and the mother of the sisters
tucked the blankets with her schooled hands
and whisked away
dust, mosquitoes, any intruder
remember this:
we each want something different
but in that first newborn week
stripped down
to the miracle
we share
we are the same
utterly
joyfully
the same

1987

The Horses

for Jenno

Like cousins
they come back
twice a year.
Invited or not.
June and September I smell them
trotting in from pasture
along the thin trail they've hooved out year after year.

With nothing but history
and mouths full of hay.
Nothing but a bridle
a saddle
a young girls' voice.

Why they return like that in dream
is why some people go back to where they grew up
just to look and drive away.

1980

Father's Day Haiku

Today Dad's biking
north towards seventy five
and a green mountain.

1999

Palestine Journal: Iron Hearts

When I was a child my grandfather on my mom's side showed me pictures of Israeli women soldiers. They were beautiful, strong; fighters for liberation. Their parents suffered the Holocaust, and they were the new generation, born to fight for freedom.

Dad's mom took me to Synagogue once in a while. She made Passover dinner, lit candles for Chanukah. My father read to me from the Old Testament.

In 1982 I became active in opposing United States/Israeli policy during the invasion of Lebanon. The idea that this brutality was being carried out in the name of Jewish people was a travesty. That it was happening was a travesty.

In 1983 I went to Nicaragua. For the first time in my life I actually saw women soldiers. Beautiful, strong women fighting for the survival of their country.

I had to go to Palestine. It seemed to me like the litmus test of our times. It seemed like when it really came down to it, if people could support Israeli policy by not acting against it, then they were against justice, against self-determination, against freedom. It seemed the ultimate contradiction. The ultimate hypocrisy. I couldn't understand why people who are so active on every other social justice issue were so quiet when it came to Palestine. I asked myself, with every worry about anti-Jewishness, is there equivalent worry about anti-Palestinianism. No. That is the crux of it.

Before leaving I received a scathing letter from a relative. It was racist against Arabs. It was arrogant, historically inaccurate and presumed that the survival of Israel was more important than anything. My mother gently implied that I didn't really understand. I knew this was hard for her and somewhere she felt I was willing to sell out my own people.

Who are my people? To me they are an international community committed to justice for all people. Not a nationality or ethnicity committed to its own survival before, after, above the survival of anyone else.

My three year old daughter held my face: *Mommy don't die.*

Even though I had a political point of view and a relative degree of understanding there was no way to know. No way to imagine. Once I got there I kept trying to compare Palestine to other situations. South Africa (under apartheid) seemed the closest. The passbooks, the no-identity, the policy of destroying people's homes and moving them by force. But finally the international community condemned the Afrikaners. Nobody says: *You have to understand. They're afraid they'll be driven into the sea.*

Who will drive them into the sea? The older woman I saw shot by a soldier on a rooftop in Nablus, just feet from us? The thirteen-year-old boy they were actually looking for? The seven-year-old girl, Lulu (*pearl* in Arabic), who went to the corner to get some milk for her mother and was shot *by accident*, who lies on a bed, can see and hear, but not talk or move? Whose parents have no health insurance and can't afford a doctor. Who lives in Gaza where there are 900 hospital beds for 700,000 Palestinians.

Soldiers are everywhere. On rooftops. At checkpoints. They are everywhere. They put up tents on rooftops to spread out. They talk by radio to the soldiers on the ground. On the roof they use binoculars. And guns.

The day after we saw the woman shot in Nablus, the newspaper said there had been shooting in Nablus. *No injuries* it read. We saw the woman bleeding. The bloody rags left on the street. We talked to the hospital director where she was finally taken. *No injuries.*

In Gaza there are laws saying Palestinians can only dig so far underground for water. Then the Israelis dig down below the law and suction out the water. The Palestinians aren't allowed to grow fruit-bearing trees. That way they can be more easily uprooted. In Gaza, in the camps, the amount of space per Palestinian, 27 square feet, is a little more than half what is recommended by the American Correctional Assocation for U.S. prisoners.

At the end of the day in Gaza, a friend said: *We have seen so much suffering. Now we have iron hearts.*

I tried to convince her and myself that we didn't have iron hearts. But it was a weak argument. We had stood around a paralyzed girl who'd been shot in the head and we didn't know what we could possibly say to her. We'd seen photos of dead children, heard stories of torture, seen demolished house bits. Who was to say, seeing and hearing and then walking away into relative safety, our hearts were not turning iron?

One man, who had been in prison fifteen years and was studying literature, said to me: *If you don't treat me like a human being. If you beat me, torture me, bulldoze my home, how can I to love you? How can I?*

How can I to love you. My people.

A Palestinian woman in Liid, inside Israel, said to us: *How can we like America? We see the soldiers (Israeli), and their uniforms and guns. We know where they come from. But we know the difference. We know the people are in solidarity with us.*

The Salvadoran mother had said this. The Nicaraguan mother. Our country is the official enemy of the mothers of the world. But we could never tell this mother weeping as she spoke to us, through her strength, saying she can't live like this; that we can't promise the solidarity of even our own community in the U.S. That this is different. That we look at each other and wonder who will talk, who will listen, and if they will be willing to go to the heart of it. Will anyone talk about U.S. aid, the millions of U.S. dollars going to Israel each year, the weapons?

In Beita, for collective punishment the authorities bulldozed seventeen homes. And then adjacent ones fell automatically. Acres of olive and almond trees were uprooted. A man there said: *How can I explain to you? It is unimaginable. Who would believe there was anybody living on earth like this? I'd rather be in prison.*

The worst, he said, *was when they took my daughter. Right in front of my eyes. That was the worst.* All his children were in prison. We saw where the stairs had been. There were a few still standing, cement steps out there in the middle of dust and nothing. Out there for only God to see. Leading to where? Out there in the naked sun he had a plastic sheet over a stick, an old sofa, a portrait, some flowers in a clear vase. *You've forgotten us,* he said. *America has forgotten us. Please come in and sit down.*

We sat with a young Palestinian woman and her two year old son in a camp between Hebron and Jerusalem. She was studying sociology and psychology. The trouble is that Arab universities had been closed since the Intifada began. Her husband was in prison. That morning her brother-in-law was taken. The military comes into her home sometimes five times a day. We were sitting talking and we heard a shot. The little boy jumped and screamed, his whole small body stiffened. How could I help but think of my three year old at home?

Before leaving the camp the woman showed us a small building where, with international support, they're making a dental clinic and a childcare center. Spotless in the middle of rubble.

We went to an Israeli settlement above Hebron and talked to a young schoolteacher. We saw the clean, well kept buildings and ground after walking past open sewers in the camps and in Liid. We asked her if she travels to the village. She told us yes.

We asked if there were problems with the Arabs. She said yes, sometimes they throw rocks. What happens then, we asked. Then sometimes the Israelis will shoot a gun in the air. She told us that when an Arab kills an Israeli nothing happens but when an Israeli kills an Arab he is punished severely. We wondered why the prisons were filled with Palestinians.

We asked where the Arabs live. *I don't know.*

Do they live in refugee camps.

I think so......

Do you think they like living there?

I think so......

Do the mothers like living with their children with no water.

I think so.

What was here before we asked her.

Nothing.

If you have no rights to water. If you have a passbook that doesn't allow you in certain places and shows if you've been in prison. *An identity card with no identity, not Israeli, not Jordanian, not Palestinian. "Who am I?"* one man asked. Who am I? If your home is bulldozed. If 90% of the youths under the age of twenty have been imprisoned. If there is military law. If you are tortured. If you can't go to school. If you can't get to a doctor. If you are not who you are because the name of who you are is forbidden. If you live in a filthy, stench-filled camp surrounded by soldiers with guns and barbed wire. If when you lived there before it was stolen it was nothing. If you are ten years old and a boy and you threw a stone or look like a boy who threw a stone or stood next to a boy who might have thrown a stone or are out of breath or have dirt on your hands or are the older woman standing next to the boy who might have thrown a stone, you are in danger.

On the plane ride going home I spoke to two young Israeli men, one just out of the military. He said ideally there should be two states but insisted that if there was a Palestinian state Israel would be invaded. Justifying the occupation. I asked him if he really thought the Palestinian people could be sacrificed. How could you, I asked.

Because I am the strong one, he said. *And I prefer it that way. Wouldn't you? If you and I were the only ones left in the world,* he asked me, *who would you choose to live, me or you?*

I thought of war. I thought of my three year old daughter

laughing and playing and holding my face before I left saying: *don't die Mommy, don't die.*

I thought of the teacher in Hebron who said: *They call it a Middle East problem. It's not a Middle East problem. It's the Palestinian problem.*

I thought of the man whose house had been demolished. When he tried to rebuild it the authorities bulldozed it again and to really punish him they blew up his water tank.

I thought of the family with the chicken cooperative. Soldiers came, killed a farmer in the field, then poured water over the stove so the women couldn't bake bread.

I thought of iron hearts.

I saw Lulu's face. Lulu, pearl. Her brown eyes sunk into mine; I stroked her brow. I couldn't think of anything to say to this seven year old girl who went out for milk and was shot in the head with a gun my tax dollars paid for. She made a muffled cry. Her eyes. All I could think to say was: *Goodbye Lulu. Goodbye.*

Upon my return I received another letter from the same relative. I understood. She had visited Israel, the Jews' promised land. I visited Occupied Palestine. Two different countries.

I am hanging a tapestry in my three year old daughter's bedroom. It is a gift from friends in the West Bank, and says: *There's no place like home.* I'm trying to explain it to her. About home. About not having one. About someone taking your home. Your water. About water.

I will never forget. I will not shut up.

Ask me who my people are. I met one of them in Israel. She is an Israeli attorney who defends Palestinians. She decided *not being something* is not enough. You must plow forward head and heart, tired feet first, towards justice. And still laughing. She was falling asleep when we met. *I'll sleep two hours then work some more* she laughed. She's going to change her country.

She's not alone. I've met her before. Anywhere in the world. Somewhere. She's very much alone.

Ask me who my people are. They are Palestinian women and children and men struggling to survive and to claim what is theirs. Land. Water. Dignity. Home. Home. Home.

They are women and children and men anywhere demanding and claiming home.

Ask me who my people are. They are Jews unwilling to succumb to paranoia and hatred, rejecting the notion that any people could possibly be superior to other peoples, as they did in the U.S. civil rights movement. As we have as a people so many times throughout history. Jews courageous enough to speak the truth and not tolerate cruelty, turning the horror of the past into understanding.

If you and I were the only ones left in the world do you really think I would choose for you to die and me to live? What kind of life would that make?

How could you even formulate such a question?

What would I be choosing?

1990

originally published in New Directions for Women, Palestine Focus *and* The East Hampton Star

3.

Not a
Protest Poem/
A Love Song

In The Middle of the Night in July

Fireflies grab the night
kissing the field of Queen Anne's Lace.
Stars shake and skid over the lake.
We don't have much time.
Unloading begins at the docks. Dreams first.
The moon guides the stragglers out,
spilling light over the water.
If you're not willing to give something up,
don't come here.

The dreams are mean
because they never stop.
Because they tell too much and someone
is always leaving. Because they are
always right. They are mean
because they are tireless and I tire
easily. Because they come back
and the untrustworthy come back
with candles and ammunition
and our language glistens in their mouths like razors.

Because they tell what but not
how. And my childhood friend appears
with her mother, cameras swinging, saying:
This isn't worth photographing.
This meeting, this memory lapse and lapse of love,
this eclipse. This tempest.
I can't iron but I can fold I repeat.
Who are you anyway, the woman in the corner asks.

What does it matter, I say, *we are trying*
to stop a war, isn't that what we're trying to do here?

The fish suck in air through their sides,
flip-flop, hooked and flung in a net.
Coyotes howl at the shifting light
and I think it's my own voice
escaping from dream.
I hear thunder and imagine: bombs.
I hear fireworks and imagine: bombs.
Across the lake, smoke; across the ocean,
borderlines, smoke. What I don't hear
I imagine.

Sparrows clip the treetops.
Clusters of leaves
hold the sky's breath in a cradle.
Harriet's laughter rows us safely to shore.
The moon returns orange.
We are beyond asking.
Now we must learn to invent.

1982

Negotiations

Don't tell me about my people
in this sunset driven moonlit night:
you'll always find sand and water
and light stripping the sky
but what cannot be conjured
out of the soaked earth
or plucked from above
is trust: the heat
of two hands meeting, a nod,
bodies hugging in awkward human silence.
The sea can soothe me
with its salt and motion
but it cannot make an oath.
Don't tell me about my people
or your loyalty.
Don't tell me about careful
or inflammatory.
I am a beast on two legs.
Anything more
or less is betrayal.

1982

For Haiti

after the floods

Standing at the harbor
in autumn morning starkness
I think I can see
across miles of water

think I can hear
the voice
of *Radio Haiti*
laughing through salt
ashes in the sea.

She is *ouverture*
daughter of the deepest cove
vodou   Toussaint
she sings *Mozambique,*
vocal chords pull across all time,
Saint Domingue,

paints *soleil,*
sapphire, moon orange fish
below the reef,
azure riplets, a boat,
she is *Gonaives,*
histoire.

She gasps,
the sinking
swollen body bubbles
nightmare blue
as if the rain were blood
pouring down
fighting for air, simply air

wilting waves of hair
wrenching locks
red brown braids Carib ink
conga
macandals float
where green is gone.

Waters once prayed for
to quench the empty dust
thirsty dream
drench to death now
as if the rain were history

history of agronomy
history of treachery
history of unshackling
the singular history
of being *Ayiti.*

I read the numbers
look for names
counting   counting
treeless air
turn my faucet on
soak by choice
face the sea

water the lover
water the savior
water the stalker
water the warrior and the war
eats homes not made of gold.

Who dies, who can flee, who is left behind?
A young girl smiles a festival of stars at night,
fights her way through mud and muck,
the terror of each day:
This is what we know.

Angels
come
and kiss a salve of light
on this beloved land
worked so long.
Angels
come to earth,
name it *Haiti, Ayiti.*

September, 2004

Not A Protest Poem/ A Love Song

After August 29, 2004*

The mothers
standing on the bridge
untie the kerchiefs
from their heads.

Their children paddle the river home in carved canoes
returned whole.

Fernando Suarez de Solar
follows the shadow of his son
his heart hanging out of his chest.
We wade in the water of his flooded eyes.

He tells his story again and again and again
into microphones, steel cameras
into the arms of strangers.

He lost his son.
There is no *why* here
only Fernando walking through crowds,
his words lining his face,
the map the marines never drew.

Where can the silence be
when we are called to speak.
Please let me find the stillness
where words begin
and let that stillness speak for me.

August, 2004

*On August 29, 2004 thousands marched through New York City to protest President George W. Bush's policies, during the time of the Republican National Convention.

Letter to the Editor

Dear friend: I must have been mistaken
to mourn those lives lost
without the proper data or permission
to accurately claim them:
real, necessary, losses at all?
I must have been out of my head
to feel a responsibility
for a people without a place to live
hunted down by my people
who were without a place to live
hunted down.

Dear editor: I know it is wrong
in the technological age
to speak from the heart
with inadequate documentation —
shall I send a human limb wrapped in brown paper
or tape record overseas phone calls
with the sound of human wailing?

Dear readers: I know I had no right
from far away, without a degree
in war, weaponry or even history
to indicate there is any way to peace
but war.

Blood answers blood.
We live in the body of our history,
drink the blood of our ancestors
and it is preposterous I know to think

we might harden
towards those who resemble us
in their fears
like the child beaten by her mother
and she watches herself growing again
and sees something so familiar
in that young face, in a gesture,
so terrifying that her impatience and fury

rise in her
like a jackhammer
for all she suffered, for all she lost and endured.
Without quite knowing what she is doing
her arms let loose across her child's face
and back and legs
as if the beating could unleash her past
and she hates herself for hurting
who she loves
and she hates who she loves
for reminding her
and the guilt and anger
gather within her
the energy to do it again.

Dear historian: Please show me
the legacy of proof
tangible as barbed wire,
the failure of imagination
that has brought us here.

Dear lover: we are talking about
necessary defense strategies,
remember when you were afraid to say:
I love you?

1982

Bill

for Margie

1. (1995)

I love
the way you laugh
at your enemies
the way
you looked
at your wife
when you ordered the black outfit
from the New York Times
knowing just how it would drape
over her small shoulders

the world knows
Attica Wounded Knee Chicago
Jackson and Kent State
but maybe the world
needs to drink
your vigor
like a tonic
and understand
struggle
as passion for living
your barritones
a lifeline
for the barricades
fear
a verb you couldn't conjugate
a noun you couldn't swallow.

Bill, when I met Fidel
watched his tapered fingers
swirl
with intelligence
in the conference room
in Havana
I couldn't help thinking of you
shooting sonnets
on any given topic
I looked everywhere

the day you died
for the one on our fridge
titled *Senate Judiciary Committee*
instead I found

a picture of you
leaning over Jon
and Billie Jean
at our baby shower
your eyes
and hands
giving birth
right there

2. (2006)

when I was 20
looking through the wisteria window
of our tiny Gay Street apartment
a family arrived
handsome booming famous attorney
stunning, brilliant mother (attorney)
one baby, one on the way

a few years and
Sarah and Emily were hanging out on the stoop
beguiling, taunting
anyone who dared share the block
Sam your dog holding court from one end of
our bite sized street to the next
undercover agents staked out at Christopher and Waverly
like bookends

no more witch hunts
talking Nicaragua
fight the right
a glass of wine on the steps in summer
when village life busted out —
Margie and I scheming...

Now it's ten years since this story-filled church soaked up your largeness
people came from everywhere
a man from Ohio
misty-eyed, told me:
He never asked, just showed up
when we needed him
and stayed.

Bill
look at the girls now
every day they re-make the world
exact, brilliant, gorgeous
daring truth the way as wily kids
they dared neighbors on our block.
A parent's dream.
Daring truth

for William Moses Kunstler Racial Justice Awards
Cathedral of St. John the Divine, NYC, June, 2006

When the Killing of a Stranger Means the World

*The Execution of Gary Graham, Shaka Sankofa,
June 22, 2000,Huntsville, Texas, U.S.*

This morning I choose no human music.
The birds work their early tour.

I interpret
looking for a message

listening for the warrior call.

I want to let you know how strong I am
that I understand the long road.

But as with any amputation,
meticulous, pre-meditated,
there is the gnawing pain,
the talking absence.

This is the story of one Black man in America,
his last breath, one eye open,
proclaiming innocence.

When we open our eyes at daybreak
hoping it didn't happen,
that eye waits for us.

We never forget
the proclamation of innocence.
We've lost our innocence.

It could be he'd killed.
It could be he'd been killed so many times before.

Could be he was a bad guy.
Could be he changed.
It could be no one wins.

With each execution
we lose a piece
of ourselves.

We do not lose
our memory.

June, 2000

Chip Chip Chip

It is natural to stand or walk and share your point of view in the place where you live. That's what a group of us did, organized so well by the East End Coalition for Peace & Justice on Tax Day, April 15, 2006, pointing to the economic and human cost of the U.S. war and occupation of Iraq. Five of us, including my nineteen-year-old daughter and her best friend, were arrested and handcuffed for walking with signs about the war and images of soldiers who've been killed. Walking, barely. Not marching, not shouting, not blocking traffic or people's ability to move on the sidewalk and shop. This seems such a small, such a meek action in the face of what has and is taking place in our names with our tax dollars.

I have engaged in nonviolent civil disobedience and will again. I have blocked traffic and made noise and will again. But that is not what we did on April 15th 2006 in East Hampton, New York.

As long as I can — breathe, talk, move — it's my duty to exercise my rights, to speak for what I believe is right and against what is wrong, to participate in democracy. That's how I was raised. That's how this country was raised. That's what the Constitution and the Bill of Rights tell us. Participate. Get in the way of injustice. It is not a secret that the war in Iraq has been built on untruths. Policies like the Patriot Act aimed at silencing the people of this country are based on a campaign of misinformation and fear. It is not a secret that the majority of the people of this country and around the world are horrified and ashamed of the arrogance and brutality of this administration's policies, from the invasion and occupation of Iraq, to the detainment and torture at Guantanamo, Abu Ghraib and prisons in Afghanistan, to the abandonment and racism of Katrina.

What is surprising is that vast numbers of people are not in the streets all the time demanding change.

The young people in our group said this about the experience: "We didn't do anything wrong. We walked down Main Street silently holding signs against the war... We recently spent several days working in the 9th Ward in New Orleans. We've seen the neglected disaster. Billions of dollars are going for war and occupation, senseless killing. That money is needed in New Orleans, the Gulf Coast and all the impoverished, neglected communities in our country. As young people we are terrified when we look at the education system and don't understand how we can be spending billions of dollars for war when there are schools without basic materials here."

In the face of today's realities, walking down a lovely village street on a beautiful Saturday with signs against a war that has and will mark this country and the world for decades to come, seems almost inconsequential. I had been thinking that — in the face of bombing and maiming, lost families and places, the people whose rights have been truly abducted and erased; what does it mean, a few of us in East Hampton? But I was reminded by a friend, a professor and local leader, that this is exactly the way rights disappear. Chip chip chip. The seeming small infractions that one might attempt to forget or explain away, the temptation to disassociate, the peeling away of our rights that leads to us one day waking up and not being able to express ourselves at all.

We can't afford, for ourselves, but more for those who can't speak, because they've been killed, or their spirits have been killed, or they are terrorized, or never really had rights; because they'd lose their jobs, or their homes, because they're still too young but they will inherit whatever mess we leave; we can't afford to let any inch of our rights be whittled away. One day we might walk down the street nodding to one another afraid to open our mouths and utter one word for fear it would be the wrong word. Or blindfolded. Or only allowed to walk on certain streets at certain times. Or only some of us. Or only one language. One color. The book Visa For Avalon, written by Bryher in 1965, tells a story about rights disappearing without people realizing what's happening, set in a seaside resort, and was reissued last year by Paris Press because of its prescience.

Rights are like muscles. Unless we exercise them they atrophy. Democracy's like that. We are engaged in an ongoing exercise of our rights to speak and walk and express ourselves and to figure out much more powerful ways to stop this war, this stain on history, and to lift up the blanket of intimidation this administration has dropped on our country, that has filtered to every small village. To exercise democracy. That's our job.

April, 2006

Just Another Day

for Herman, for Grace and for Leslie

Like an overgrown cheerleader
or an over zealous Mom at a first recital
I beamed in the afternoon rain
at the high school kids who walked out on war.

In the evening, I sat in my living room
by a fire with assembled
"poets for peace,"
dogs scratching and barking at the bedroom door.
We ate the homemade cake
the kids laced in purple icing spelling the day's title:
"poets for peace"
which originally was
"poets against the war."

The phone on the couch rang,
my Dad calling, cell phone
in the Washington Square Park air
a roar of raucous human possibility
crackled through technology:
Can you hear Leslie?
he shouted into the phone
Can you hear — ten thousand people!

I held the phone up for the poets to hear,
my Dad faded into the thrill of collective hope in a crowd.

Children carried a globe through the streets of New York
in February when the World Said No To War
and the mayor and police said no to marches
so the children walked the globe through Manhattan
instead of leading the march.
When a piece of it ripped
a girl called for help:
We have to fix the world!

My father and I
are not simply for peace
(not that there's anything simple about peace).
We're against this war
and all that dragged us here.

I first learned these things from him
when I was thirteen
and he used his skill and art to try to stop another war.

I find myself talking to strangers these days
saying things like:
It's a beautiful day to work for peace!
wondering what kind of Mr. Rogers
or go-go-over-the-hill-no-shame-mom-for-peace
I've become.

My kids think I'm weird
dancing around the house
into the dialectic.

I wore pink (panties) and a pink orange scarf
on March 8th International Women's Day
to support women trying to prevent war
but truly, my sisters, I am wearing
a red flowing chiffon top
purple suede pants that grip,
high heeled boots to make a mark
a large blue United For Peace & Justice button
on this thigh that runs four miles a day.

I want to sit with a glass of full bodied red wine,
put my boots up,
look into intelligent and compassionate eyes,
a strong warm hand hinting at my middle aged hip,
and just soak
in
poetry.

March, 2003

Ambition

I want to write a poem
that will move you beyond caring.
A poem that makes you laugh,
the air between your ribs
holding court in your body.
A poem that makes you cry till your face crunches up
and shoulders shake
large above your arms.
A poem that makes you pee in your pants,
that will make you
think, that is
its own original thought.
I want to write a poem
that's more than a meal,
more than shelter
that turns your world
inside out.
I want to write a poem
that hurts to see.
I want to write
an irresistible poem
that makes you squirm
leaves a hickey
on your skin
the kiss you can't wipe off.
I want this poem
to be universal health insurance,
full employment,
to stop an execution.
I want this poem to pay poets.
I want this poem to be more than
affirmative action
more than anti-racist,
something we haven't named
that hasn't slipped off our lips
in meeting after meeting.

I want this poem to be something
even truth can't define.
I want this poem
to spread around money
not like a dirty diaper
but like what it is.
I don't want to manipulate you
I want you desperate
to go there with me.
I want this poem
to transport my passion
into power.

1994

Prelude

*In loving memory of Safiya Henderson-Holmes
and Ingrid Washinawatok*

We do fight terror with beauty.

In Matagalpa, Nicaragua
on a hillside
mothers of fallen children
threw doves on us
as we walked into their Casa de Madres
took each of us by the hand, twelve different U.S. women,
led us to a monument surrounded by grass
to place flowers on stones for their sons and daughters,
turned to say: *please, sisters,*
tell your president
to stop killing our children.

We fight terror with beauty and humor.

In El Salvador
after beatings
young women in prison
on crutches that didn't fit
bellies empty from hunger strike
dressed up, made up,
stomped around,
performed as *the enemy* for guests
from another America.

Don't forget us they called
as we walked out of the prison gates.

We fight terror with beauty
and with tilling
tilling of memory, tilling of land.

Near Ramallah on the West Bank
women in a farm cooperative
sewed seeds in ancient soil.
In Gaza, bursts of red pink rose from sewers,
embroidery spilling out over delicately crafted patches of fabric
spelling: *no place like home.*

84

We fight terror
when a door is opened.

In a South Bronx homeless shelter
women welcomed
and embraced
visitors from Israel, Palestine, Egypt, Turkey
as bombs burst down on Baghdad,
sharing cookies and a drink.
No place like home.

We fight terror with thought.

In Cuba
during what they called the *special period*
when the lights went out
someone told me: *I used that time when the elevator stopped
to think, to imagine, grateful to be alive.*

We fight with harmony.

Becky Genia of Shinnecock Nation
sat on the turned-over sacred land
as bulldozers for the Parrish Pond Subdivision
roared through.
Her voice
like the water surrounding the reservation
singing forever

2001

Here's Why

Because the red hibiscus
might bloom
only once

Because the resonance
of understanding
might disappear
leaving notes from a meeting
on paper
not lines on a face
or breath of work

Because the young girl's arc
stuns the crystal morning
Wrist to thigh
sun-stroked wood into sky
torso to the heavens
she takes the world
thirsty
without measure

Because to un-name is to fly

Because we have only
each other

1996

4.

Will I Have
The
Courage?

My Election Journal/ Will I Have the Courage?

George W. Bush 2nd Term, U.S., November 2004

"...And because revolution always takes place on the basis of great hope and rising expectations, I am not too worried about the future. One way or another, a whole lotta change is gonna come..."
    ©1998 June Jordan from the essay "On the Night of November 3, 1992" *Affirmative Acts: Political Essays* **Anchor/Doubleday Books**

* * *

Wednesday November 3rd, 2004, 7 a.m.

I walk to a Starbucks in midtown Manhattan. The tv was on all night. Ghosts in a ghost town. An outpost. Should we secede? Along with the other non slave pre-civil war Blue states. The young woman behind the counter smiles sweetly: "are we a little sad today?" I've become a stereotype, dark crescent moon outlines under my eyes, a little grey showing in my out-of-control hair, buttons announcing my beliefs pinned on my multi-colored child's backpack and red Charlie's Angels jacket. I engage with strangers about the state of the world or their cool Converse hi-tops. It drives my thirteen-year- old crazy — *a political comment about everything Mom*! So predictable. All the subtleties of my silent poet heart submerged in the terror of the day, my sense of inadequacy and horror pushing me to weirdness. Sometimes I try to stop myself from asking strangers how they feel about the war, who they are voting for and isn't justice a nice word. The sympathetic woman getting my latte and taking my $3.95 at Starbucks on this eerie November 3rd still has life in her face. She's young, Black and it's New York, so when the lines around my mouth begin to twitch like they did when, as a child, I was overcome with sadness in public, even as I try to hold them in place, I feel safe, comforted by her youth. On the lampposts, muddied, torn stickers. On the streets, tired old leaflets. Remnants, like lost children, our words, drifting specks. Signs of life. I try to read each set of eyes on the windy lightless street. Every face seems blood drained, walking transfusions, all colors are business — grey, tan, black. The magenta, orange of autumn gone with the surreal sudden blush of midafternoon expectation less than twenty-four hours earlier. It feels like Warsaw to me. It feels like Berlin. It feels like an urban Western in the East after the bad guys rode into town. It feels like the movie I won't pay money to see.

* * *

The part of our country we have lost, we lost long ago. Or never had. (My arrogance and time-spent allows me to say "we.") What we have gained, is even more of us, more organized. Almost half the country. (I keep repeating as if to believe it — if only the world had voted.) Waves of engaged citizenry of all ages sweeping across the country to knock on doors, coalesce beyond the differences that usually separate us.

* * *

We have always believed that if people had information, saw the lies, the pain of policies, they would demand change; that self interest, jobs, health care, housing, come top on the list. Then what we call morality, repugnance at unjust war, killing, torture. There seems to be a basic flaw in that organizing principle. A lack of acknowledgement of the human condition, the reality of two people presented with the same information reacting completely differently. The reality of conflicting perceptions and definitions of what it means to be human. Our way of thinking has presumed the innate goodness of people. Presumed that information is a clear and direct thing. Not so clear. Not so clear as Clear Channel. People want authority, answers, a common enemy, a confident father, God. Don't necessarily value thought. When father batters, look away. Blame the battered. Call it protection. Call it strong. Call it confident. Become a batterer.

* * *

A virus in the eye. Use the other eye. Lose sight in both eyes. June Jordan wrote at the end of her essay "Problems of Language in a Democratic State": "...I believe that somebody real has blinded America in at least one eye. And, in the same way that so many Americans feel that 'we have lost our jobs,' we suspect that we have lost our country..."

* * *

August, 2004

In August just before the Republican National Convention and the temporary liberation of New York City (protest city regardless of no park permit), I ran into the Secretary of State riding my bike to the beach to watch my daughter surf. I rode up to him in my blue jean skirt and "all of us or none" cap, no one else in sight on the quaint country road. This is what we said, more or less:

I asked him if he was who I thought he was. He said probably. I asked if we could talk for a minute. What do you want to talk about he asked. I said I thought he had a chance to make history. He said how. I said he could switch and stand for another president. He said I was silly, just silly. (I've been called naïve, hopelessly optimistic, "heartfelt" as a poet, but never silly!) I said no I wasn't silly, just hopeful. I said I was worried about the war. He said we were bringing elections and democracy to two places — Afghanistan and Iraq, but people like you (me) don't care about that. I asked what he would tell the mothers of the killed soldiers about the bombs and the fact that the war isn't what we were told. He said he would tell them it's a big sacrifice but it's worth it. He said people like you (me) never think there's a reason to bomb. I said he shouldn't assume about people (like me). I asked if he thought people ever changed their minds about important issues, based on information (prompted by my sister's brilliant essay on the subject). He said you (I) might but he wouldn't. I said I was worried about our own democracy. He said he had been working with our democracy more than thirty years and it is strong. And we will win he said. People will vote in Afghanistan and Iraq, he said, but you (me) don't care about that. We will win he said and then turned into a driveway. Thanks for talking to me I said.

* * *

Tuesday November 2, 2004, election day

I sat at lunch in Bucks County, Pennsylvania with our United For Peace & Justice posse, on duty under the direction of ACT (America Coming Together), mostly workers from the health care union-1199, between sweeps of suburban door knocking in what J. called *getting out the beemer (BMW) vote*! There we were, a table of middle-aged progressive activists — gay and straight, East Indian and American Indian, Jewish, women and one guy — teachers who are organizers and organizers who are teachers, who, like so many thousands, had joined together with the vast stream of moderate to moderately liberal to reformed and pissed off Republican to hard core progressives in an extraordinary act of faith and determination to vote for a party that had long since lost direction and certainly abandoned us, and a candidate who, regardless of a surprisingly decent voting record, didn't offer an alternative on the war or much of anything. We weren't voting for the party or the candidate but our souls and some time for the world. Many of us had long since given up on the Democrats. But history and the reality of war called.

At lunch I learned from the eighth grade teacher and only male among us, about Bonobos. Chimp-like, these nearly extinct monkeys from Central Africa engage in more sex than any other primate and for a longer period of their lives. Bonobo society is sexually egalitarian; males and females have equal power and they each have sex with both genders. The female has the largest labia of any other primate, as a result of use. When a fight is in the making, Bonobos have sex instead. Had the saying *Make Love Not War* come from an anthropologist, not pot-smoking electric-guitar-playing long-haired anti-heroes, would it have been taken as a real alternative?

Throughout the day we received bulletins from our comrades around the country: Ohio, Philadelphia, Florida, Michigan, New Mexico. As nearly half of the people in this country did, we went from anxious excitement in the mid to late afternoon to breath holding as we headed out after the polls closed into the darkness of the highway through the smoke of New Jersey, towards our city, the one that had watched those planes dive into buildings and insisted on no war. Our state won. The beemer, rapper and black church votes delivered the mandate for sanity. *Have we been living in a bubble?* J. put her head in her hands in the seat next to me as we searched map-quest, the road home and radio news.

The night before as we anxiously ate huge bowls of spaghetti at a family Italian Restaurant on the highway in Bucks County, our lovely young waitress confided that indeed she was excited to vote for the first time, and as a teacher, she had decided to vote for Bush, as her Dad would, because she didn't like the *Leave No Child Behind* Act and didn't think Kerry would stop it either. That's exactly what she said. J. brilliantly, gently offered a different perspective about children being left behind. As we were leaving A. saw her, kneeling, next to an older woman who was telling her about *the devil and partial birth abortions*. I kept hearing A.'s voice as we walked from one large suburban house to the next: *How can we change this country?* she implored. *When people live this way and are blind to the fact that it is off the backs of the rest of the world.* She is from India and for a year had been living and working in the woods there learning about medicinal herbs. Her challenge is not a new idea to me. I've worked with women from Haiti, South Africa, the Middle East, Central America, the Caribbean ... Mississippi... I live with it everyday in eastern Long Island where newly arrived Central and South Americans clean houses, pick weeds and can't get a driver's license, vote or afford to buy a home.

* * *

Just after 7 a.m. Wednesday, Nov. 3, 2004

I walk to my car looking at each person I pass like a family member.
This is New York after all, city of burned towers, Amadou Diallo,
Families for a Peaceful Tomorrow, the Health and Hospital Union
1199, the 85% majority. This crying town is the capital of the world.
And the world is crying.

On the Long Island Expressway east towards home, green ocean
waves I'll never again take for granted, and my beautiful, funny
girls; coming home from the battleground state of Pennsylvania via
beloved war torn Manhattan, I open the windows wide, let in all
carbon monoxide, the "Essential Leonard Cohen" blaring monotone
romantic words about poverty, racism, war and the woman he
loves. Banners over the highway read: *Sandy loves Tommy. Support
Our Troops. Remember 9/11.*

Then I cry. A big open-windowed gushing. To get it out before I
see the girls. Before I see another human. Or even a deer in the
driveway or our dog Luna. To get it out before I look at the perpetual
sea or my beautiful house wondering how I deserve a beautiful
house. Before I check e-mail, kitchen sink or bills. Before I see my
eighty-year-old sprinting mother who spent two days getting out
votes with the NAACP in Florida, and thinks I'm always optimistic.
Before I see the father of my beautiful girls who is making mosaics
and fiercely planting things in the earth, whose ninety-one-year-
old father died quietly just days before the so-called election but
not before seeing the Red Sox win. I run through years in my mind.
Coffee and dancing in Nicaragua. The day Mandela was released.
Bombs over Lebanon. The day the Sandinistas lost. Grenada in a
flash. Haiti burning. First Gulf war and Military Families. Press
releases, endless press releases. The Palestinian mother hearing
her daughter's voice crying outside the prison walls as ice was
pressed on her milk-filled breasts. Taina, of *Make The Road By
Walking*, thanking Hillary Clinton for forgetting poor women. Chile.
Swimming in a river in Cuba. Ingrid's assassination in Colombia,
South America. Neruda. Always Neruda. The deaths of friends who
would have helped make the poem we need today.

Without them the highway is vast and lonely. My own terror
doesn't distinguish between death by cancer, burning Constitution,
Fallujah, virus in the eye.

* * *

What is the real name of this country? Is it *Sandy loves Tommy*? Or
Support our Troops? Is it Christian or White Christian? Is it Fear
of Sexuality? Or is it The Gap? Maybe it's Victoria's Secret. I am
hopeless and at the same time filled with a momentary ever-rising
sense of the possible. Lazy and dutiful. Exhausted and inspired.
Lonely and not alone. I am terribly irritated by almost everything
I hear and read, each singular seemingly simplistic analysis and
declaration, as though human history, and our brief stint at it,
could be wrapped up in a glib byline; and at the same time I gasp
at the very fact of air and trees and daughters, the energy of the
almost majority, the horizon of legacy, serene in my long view.

* * *

When E was three, before I went to Palestine she took my face in
her chubby little hands and said: *Don't die Mommy, don't die.* I heard
that voice through every check point, bulldozed home and mother's
story. Now I want to say to the threads of democracy, inadequate as
they are, I want to say to reason and compassion: *Don't die, don't die.*
I want to say to poetry and resistance: *Don't die.*

* * *

I cry on the highway before pretending. I, who preach emotional candor
and ever-ready activism, prepare for the mask, the tincture of hope,
the legacy, the prescription, what I will say to friends on the phone
or in email exchange or on the corner, how I will refuse to succumb
to what is being called *depression*, how amazing the effort has been,
how much we have to build with, how we will carry on in the spirit of
those who came before. I know what to say. I even know how to brush
my cheeks with blush, fluff my hair and show undying enthusiasm
to the assembled bodies in my living room or at a dwindling vigil at
the Town Square. My voice used to stay flat like the line of a hospital
heart monitor when the patient is dying. Lacking a PhD, contract with
Doubleday or a good speaking fee, I taught myself to cheerlead.

I cry with the trucks and fumes on 495 for our inadequacy as a species
to care for one another, for our failure to stop the travesty against our
own human definition. I cry for every Iraqi mother, every U.S. mother
of a soldier, brutalized child or death row inmate, every Haitian, every
woman's body, the continent of Africa and every piece of earth and river.
I cry for our language, rich as a cornfield, resilient and acrobatic in the
wind, its power shape-shifted into a goodie bag with a gun, to be shot

off and left hollow by the side of the road. Hollow hallowed language. I cry for my kids. And the kids who don't have two parents, homes and fresh food. Knowing I will stop soon. Knowing I will *put on my boxing gloves* as A.H. said. *Suck it up* as E. says. And find the beauty. Again.

* * *

Same Day, 3 p.m.

I worry about seeing the girls, those first moments, how to give them the resilient strength and sense of historic struggle I feel necessary and still be authentic. I start by apologizing for our country. Then talking about the legacy of struggle. A litany of feel- better context for my babies, my roll-call, what I live by. E., seventeen, says she is relieved. She had feared my devastation would match hers and we would sink together. I'm glad I did something right. She asks if it's ok that she's really angry. Be angry my love, I tell her. Be angry with all you've got.

* * *

I continue my silent prayer-like apology to the people of the world. Hoping someone might hear and that the hearing could be of use. And the pre-requisite pc commitment to fight on, muttering my duty like the pledge of allegiance.

* * *

Next Days

Silences, protecting the need to let air breathe on raw places. No words. Too many words. Each waking morning, a sweat, a gasp, moment of hope it didn't happen; we don't have to look straight into the daggers of deception knowing we failed to stop it. I am temporarily dispensing with the prefix *How are you?* E-mail battalions. What to forward, what not to forward, what to believe. Everything is annoying. Everything is believable; nothing is believable. Each pundit and journalist, even friends and allies, sound simplistic and arrogant to me. The *values* question, i.e. power of the Christian Right. Not *the values* question. How much *the values* question. Whose values. The misinformation issue — wmd's, safety, Al Qaeda in Iraq, whose safety? Fraud. Tampering. Intimidation. Cover up. The votes still don't add up. They might add up. Whose votes. The pre civil war slave states map. Lies, lies. Bad campaign, terrible campaign. Great GOTV (get out the vote). Bad breath. I think e-mail was invented to make us feel we are doing something during the Age of Un-enlightenment.

I don't have a clue what to do. And I fear (don't tell, please) that the temporary fragile glorious mosaic created these last months will shatter into thousands of shards like a stained glass chandelier if we're not very careful. And smart. And caring.

* * *

I will read Natalia Ginzburg on fascism in Italy 1939-44. I will read Nadine Gordimer on apartheid. I will read Marquez. I will read Baldwin. Neruda always. William Butler Yeats, Walt Whitman, Langston Hughes. Du Bois. I will read Darwish, Shihab Nye, Amichai, Said. Frederick Douglass. Blanche on Eleanor. And of course June Jordan. Read, read, read. Who am I kidding! No time to read.

* * *

I turn to my friends with collars and holy waters to explain at least part of the phenomenon. The same thing happens, it seems, in the church as in the Democratic party — everyone's afraid to tell what they know, or even know what they know.

* * *

If Fernando Suarez de Solar of Military Families Speak Out, who wears his dead son's face on his chest, killed in Iraq, walked through the rivulets of this vast untied country talking to people in a place called Heart Land would things change? Would minds change because hearts could not stay closed? When information is locked out of the mind, can the heart open?

* * *

I think we should have same sex marriages all over the place all the time. Regardless of who sleeps with whom, regardless of who has the license to marry people, regardless of my belief that the law has no place in relationships. Just marry. In public. Everywhere. And we need to run people for office in every local and state election.

* * *

I don't want to say out loud: *witch hunt.* What will happen here now? We will all be put to the test. Will I have the courage, the clarity, the fortitude? What is safety to one is terror to another. What is *other?* This country is polarized in at least four ways. If more than eighty-eight% of African Americans voted for Kerry (even with the churchgoers who were swayed by the evangelicals), and the majority of African Americans have been and are against the war, and the successful intimidation and voter intervention targeted Black and Latino communities, and the map lines up... do the math. Du Bois ever- prescient.

* * *

OK: just for the record: Bad Factors: 1. Christian Right aka fundamentalism, aka ordinary people give over their minds and participate in widespread abdication and cruelty aka fear same sex and abortion more than bombs and no jobs (how does this happen and what can we do about it); 2. campaign of fear and lies 3. no Democratic party or program or campaign; 4. Fraud, intimidation, racist intervention 5. Pre civil war slave state matches 2004 vote; 6. Schools more interested in tests than learning.

Good Factors: 1. GOTV mania/zillions take it on the road, the e-mail express, computerized phone campaigns, door knocking; 2. great numbers of good lawyers protecting our rights 3. Michael Moore keeps us laughing; 4. George Soros keeps giving; 5. MTV, Eminem, The Boss, Stevie Wonder, rappers; 6. the organizing: United for Peace & Justice, Count Every Vote, Young Voter Alliance, Global Exchange, Just Vote, Voter Protection, Move ON, ACT, National Voice, Black Box etc etc etc; 7. my daughter and her friends registered eighteen new voters in the lobby of the high school; 8. gatherings, protests, readings, meetings immediately after. See - adding the numbers this way, more good than bad. That's progressive education for you! In the big picture, we won!

* * *

My mom says it sounds vindictive when I say the Kerry campaign betrayed its vast constituency.

* * *

Of course the election was stolen.

* * *

I call 212 868-5545, United For Peace and Justice, report in, grateful I have somewhere to go. The name is right. This is what I need to do.

* * *

I'm not fronting now. I'm ready. Won't stop crying but will try to keep it private. Won't let those motherfuckers take our souls, keep raping. Don't know what, but together we will. I propose the Bonobo way.

November 13, 2004

5.

Conversation Between Heaven and Earth

Conversation Between Heaven and Earth

five years since I fell over the earth
forced myself to look at your made-up face in a wood box
it wasn't you
I delivered the eulogy
told how you rinsed the tomato sauce out of the spaghetti
for Naimah and Amandla
at Cummington when they were ten
you were trying to write as a mother does
Ajax in hand
Naimah has brought back your words to live forever
the story of women in prison

where are you at some ungodly hour when I need an ear for these words
can't go out there naked punctuation all crazy
you would say my clothes don't match
it is all a breaking of bars a planting of words a faith unimaginable
my arms around Naimah but I was pale she stood taller
than a young woman in your red dress taller than me
her pale aunt shrinking at that moment my voice caught
the way it did in childhood
at a gravesite
poems or beauty don't bury
when Mbachi came from Zambia people thought
she was your daughter
this is relevant don't cut this line
our survival is relevant
our stories from Edgecombe Avenue   Zambia   Buffalo
and this Narrow Lane
are relevant
if I go to another meeting where men turn from naming
every rape I will

I know nothing new
wake in terror

did I tell you Naimah is strong and open
like rivers of Egypt we never swam
but dreamed of
we have always
carried bags   banners   babies on hips   backs   bellies

rinsed tomato sauce
have always cupped our hands like moons
to catch the wet crinkly utterance of life
crashing through dripping legs remember how you raced
to my baby shower late of course but with a basket of everything
I might need for the overflow
we have always melted the metal part of burning
into resistance

I can't possibly think of a new or original thing to say
but I just turned fifty and you left us at fifty
honestly I know less
question more
remember when we wrote a poem together about where we live
the black white beige and the food   children   Marvin Gaye
death penalties your black hands which are black
my beige hands living white
victorious in the holding
defying these cancers
except oh my if only you could see the girls now
you would sigh like the sun peaking through
the most glorious dawn because they are women and they know
    things
love to dance like we did speak Spanish
traverse continents they know something
poems roll like the sea
in your red dress
both girls wrote to you their aunt
we try to teach our children living something true but contradictions
eat our insides like snickers bars
Naimah has three kids
sits at the computer with your words
her words

you wrote *everything sits on a minute*

minutes fall like Falluja
at least you didn't have to see this
I recite the litany of brave women I practiced before birth
following your verse but the names scale down my body like skin
when I say *sister* we earned that
didn't name before earth tore open
to live

we who remain
suck poetry through veins
laugh volcanoes
laugh civil disobedience
pull onions from every sauce

drink
coffee in Gaza
grateful you didn't have to see hot sauce jazz blues raped
and they gave the storm a woman's name
grateful you can't hear the bombs again going down on ancient
    alphabets
like hard body parts into soft places

forced
your body left you
the cells testifying only against life finally
who legislates

this is all I can write at this hour of my life
love poems love poems   resistance to cancer . resistance to war
resistance to stealing what we grow
resistance to leaving
resistance to hacking story like machetes

I know I need to talk about the place ghosts don't want to go
the naked place of responsibility
but all I can do is shake here in the middle of the night
in my drenching
dare the words
to come
drops of sweat and rain
orange light across our sky

I can't recall my grandmother saying the word *woman*
but that's what she gave me
my mother said *woman* told me never never let a person
with testicles lay a hand to you
come home to your mother you hear me that's the only rule

we have to do more than pray for our daughters
it is the middle of the night of my life
my sister is making fewer movies and more self defense martial arts
she has babies
and a body

I'm holding my breath saying the names of our girls
the way you would
in my pajamas at 3 a.m. no more nightgowns
in the zone as you called it

a moment on heaven still on this earth still eating tomatoes
seeds we spit out as girls
fruit we loved as women
breathing horse whiskers we can be girls we can be women
we can be colors we never imagined the prison doors just
blew open your poems did that

In memory: Safiya Henderson Holmes
December 30, 1950 — April 8, 2001

written for V-DAY Festival NYC 2006
(with thanks to Eve Ensler, Alexis De Veaux)

Prayer

1. Fall and once more the time for gathering
   the dead leaves and the green hearts
   that were buried alive, palms on palms
   under the bark, under the skin, under the breath.

   My arms are heavy.
   My fingers ache from the work of
   separating the new from the old.
   My legs work without my telling them —
   back and forth
   from tree to tree to open field
   where at last they breathe, unattached, like the stray leaves.

   In the open field there are no barriers
   between the buried and the breathing.
   All things move freely.
   I inhale and exhale without fear.

   But the gathering begins again —
   I try to place
   each small leaf, each limb, with its own face.

2. I have seen her born in springtime,
   I have grown with her, and eleven years later
   I have seen her die, a young mother, in springtime.
   I have seen her twisted foal pulled from her.
   I have stood with her and watched her die.

   Beside her grave I planted an apple tree,
   beside her dead foal, beside so much of myself.
   I see no spring this year. Only the blood,
   only the green sucked from the leaves.
   I find no breath in this still space where I lie
   on the soil, on the heartbeat.

3. I walked each day in summer, in the quiet non-birthing months,
   to stand over her grave, breath of my childhood,
   and I imagined
   her swinging towards me, her one striped hoof leading,
   one small ear pointed forward, one to the side, listening —
   the soft sweep of arc in her face,
   eyes so familiar I think they are mine.

I imagined her
lying flat, neck reaching, belly contracting,
her nostrils sucking in.
I felt her head grow heavy.

I imagined her
still.

I tried to summon up her courage
to celebrate what is not lost,
like a gardener, to spread the mulch,
the dead leaves,
over the seeds in the ground.

4. I am searching for the softest things now,
    the even stroke of a voice
    that never hears itself start or stop,
    that knows its own bareness.

    It is September
    and buds, small green palms
    translucent
    have appeared on all the trees.

1979

Second Letter to my Mother

don't ever die
I wanted to say
as you planted a tree
for your mother
in her 92nd year
resting place forever
overlooking the reservoir
on the hill she nurtured
with suffragette organic zeal
and a nineteenth century fantasy of perfection

Ella said it's okay
when someone dies
because *a new one always comes*
like that girl!
pointing to our baby

dear mom
I'm finally old enough to admit
it's never okay
when someone dies

suddenly I saw the daughter
in my mother
orphaned at sixty-seven
suddenly I wanted to mother you
small in your jeans and boots

suddenly
I saw myself a mother orphan

dear mom
I used to talk tough about death
now I look at my children
look at my mother
and pray for immortality

1992

Spring/Inheritance

in memory of my grandmother Lina

A grapefruit
or those greenhouse coddled tomatoes
nudged into ripeness by crooked fingers
with one simple silver ring

those glistening ever-so-many-times-a-day brushed teeth
eyes as clear
waiting to hear the latest little victories of an offspring
or the offspring of an offspring

maybe it's the word: *feminist*
I glommed onto
like a baby to the breast
turned into life work
recounted in writing to my daughters

maybe it's the rustling blue
or rough weavings instead of walls
tea instead of coffee
pulp filled orange juice
or a home made swimming pool like a blue egg

high decibel throat clearing:

Now tell me...
are you very busy?
what wonderful things are you doing?

My voice can't reach your enthusiasm
in the telling
my other-side-of-the-family mouth won't work that way

the wet human breath of failure
or just *not-so-wonderful*
can't find its space to sigh

Dear Lina
I smell, hear, taste
that long wood, varnished table,
apples in the bowl,
wheat germ and your husband's forbidden chocolate treasures.

I talk to the Cedar of Lebanon you gave Mom
wondering how you thought about it
and growing *Arab horses* —

our swallowed rupture leaking
Jerusalem
being two different kinds of Jews in one family.

I want to turn to you
five foot round, grand
and take your worked hands the way you took mine
that cool tomato soup summer when I worked nearby
and say

it's all right
get dirty
cry a little
fold for a second

it won't break you

look at what you've reaped!

I wrap my infant girl
in a tiny flowered cotton blanket
trimmed with satin
and tell her:

Your great grandmother made this for you
in her last making days
before she joined her flowers
and that elegant birch

Great grandmother, I tell her.
Imagine that.

Ella loves grapefruits.
She calls Justine *Justice.*
I know you can hear that.

I hear your ears ringing
defying deafness.

Spring's coming.
I expect a note charted out on that old Smith Corona
waxing blossoms and buds and birds...
an invitation.
Yes, an invitation.

1992

Prayer 2

*for Charles and Gale
and for Donald Walter Woods
December 18, 1957 — June 25, 1992*

Charles sleeps with the light on.
Gale takes showers.
I pull the covers up over my head and sweat.

We call,
fall asleep, the phone
hunched up in our shoulders.
Sigh and sing.

Grief passes through
between us
like a shawl
in an ancient dance.
It holds us folded between dusk and dawn.

We stare into it.

Our friend is gone.

Our business is words
but they don't steer us
into understanding the voiceless chair.
They *do* move us.

That's why we write
ourselves into healing.
That's why we put our stories down,
our complicated love,
like birds gathering twigs for a nest,
swift and careful.

I call Charles *Donald*,
his name escaping
involuntarily
when my lips part
like I was sleep talking.
We're expecting him still.
To speak at least.

Charles lights candles.
Gale cooks greens at ten,
takes more showers.

I exercise till my legs shake,
hold my baby — who Donald held —
cry at the soft pink sleeve over the potato field.
Unloyal beauty, not holding its breath for death.

How long do we hold our breath?
How much do we say?

Our lilies were the gayest thing at the church
Charles told me.
I didn't know that.

The delicacy of learning
a new language, landscape.
I listen for the nuance,
AIDS turning our love into a grave.
We plant flowers of words.

Beautiful weapons.

Teach each other the fragile terrain,
where to go.

Our skin colors and tongues,
childhood,
and choice of touch
alphabets apart.
We tenderly piece them together.

I ask Charles if he remembered a handkerchief.
He was beaten so much as a child
tears don't come, he told me.

So I grew into a person who can't bear
to see another person in pain.

What can we do?

Keep working.

Before separate sleepless nights,
we each turn the lights on.
In Mississippi B.J. sleeps with a light on too.

We're all afraid of the dark.

Donald
are you there?

1991

What Matters: Honoring Betty Shabazz

I had to go to Betty Shabazz's Memorial because our humanity is hanging on an edge — the meaning of our lives and the value of life itself — and any moment I have the privilege and possibility to remember what is important and what is possible and what matters, I need to do that.

I could do that. Someone else had to be somewhere else on that Sunday. For what matters. But because I could be there. I had to.

I had to go because the story gets changed. And because it's a big story. It is the story of oceans and wars and mountains and murders and cruelty and courage and abandonment. The old world and the new world and the unspeakable passage. It is the story of tyranny and heroism. And it is the story of a man and a woman and children and children's children. It is the story of different Gods and different houses of Gods. It is the story of our lives and the lives before us.

It is the story of the ones who dare speak first. And alone. In an unheard language cracking open like an egg.

I had to go to Betty Shabazz's Memorial because Independence Day can hurt.

Because Haki Madhubuti, from Chicago, talked about African America's *First Families*. I had to pay tribute to the *First Families*.

I had to go to the Celebration of Betty Shabazz because the tenderness of life requires that we hold on to our most profound love in the ways that we know how. That love can be for someone we know or a complete stranger or an idea or a vision or a commitment or an act that tells us we do in fact have infinite potential based on love and growing from love. And at the same time we are oh so fragile. Gone in a moment. Gone. And that we are still always, the lover, the sister, the brother — Mommy and Daddy. Before, after and during the big moments and gestures.

I had to go for the integrity of remembering.

Remembering can be sitting in an overflow room with a video screen at Riverside Church with the thousands. Arms outstretched. It can be in a quiet corner alone. It can be anywhere at any time.

I had to go because we talk a lot in our lifetimes. Sometimes we talk and talk and meet and meet. And talk more. Sometimes the words come and live outside in bubbles and they lose the pulse of their origin and destination. And some times are for listening. Being somewhere and just listening. The humility of listening.

Listening to Myrlie Evers-Williams talk about her *sister*. Her *girlfriend*. The private times and the fun times and the laughing times. About the public and what the public could never know or understand. Holding onto Coretta Scott King. And Coretta Scott King telling that "Daddy King" used to say if you have one good friend in your lifetime you're lucky.

I looked at the friend sitting next to me and she looked at me.

I thought of the good friends I have. And of the friends who aren't really. Who are colleagues or acquaintances. I thought of what "good friend" means. And I felt lucky. And suddenly clear. Free from the disappointment of a not really good friend. And I thought of the weight of that statement coming from where it did. Where loyalty is your life. Literally, your life.

The way it is in any war.

I had to go because people touch humanity and change the world in different ways and many are never known for how they do it or what they give, but some people change it by their largeness and their courage and their clarity and that is indisputable. And that is destiny. Those who had no real choice but to hold the world up on their hearts faced a certain way.

I had to go for the motherless daughters and the children of the motherless daughters and the dignity and beauty of the motherless daughters. And what is unknown about the motherless daughters, the secrets and the agony of the motherless daughters whose mother and father changed the world. And the words of the eldest of the motherless daughters shooting like arrows into the hearts of the thousands. Arrows holding the earth's deepest soil. Arrows bloodied with loss and unhealable wounds. Arrows from the bottom of the salt sea. Arrows from the heart that has been broken and mended and broken and mended and broken. Not by a person, but a nation. The words of the eldest of the motherless daughters shooting like the most poignant arrows a human heart could ever carry.

In her call for joining. In her passionate call for reconciliation that moves beyond any language we use when we try to speak of the unspeakable separations and isolations and insults and misunderstandings that are killing us.

And the eldest of the motherless daughters spoke of Daddy in the kitchen when Mommy was going to *get another baby.* She spoke of a love affair. And a family. This man whose *X* has been usurped. Whose words have been carved up and re-spun. This man was Daddy in the kitchen in a love affair in a family. This man who told the truth and did not die but was murdered. This motherless daughter whose words like arrows reached the hearts of the thousands this day of remembrance of what matters and the absolute human suffering because of what matters.

My sister, an educator, talks about teaching children about *what matters.*

Dr. Betty Shabazz was a nurse and an educator and a mother and an activist and the bearer of a legend and a Black woman in an America about which her husband dared tell the truth and for which his life was stolen and about which she told the truth and she mattered and what she did in her life mattered and the way she did it mattered.

I had to go not because I'm a particular color or language or checkbook or worshiper but because of having borrowed this space on earth for this time and the richness of that borrowing and knowing who else has borrowed and who has paid. Or as David Dinkins said *who is in arrears.*

I had to sit with Margie Ratner and Emily Kunstler who are Bill's wife and daughter and my family too and oh so quietly think what we were thinking and feel Bill's presence who walked with those husbands of those wives and stood arm in arm with them and represented them legally and represented her daughter when she needed it. As we sat in the overflow room at Riverside Church where Mrs. Evers-Williams and Mrs. King stood cloaked in each other and history, their sister absent. Their legends flowing like blood and water through the veins of the great Church and into the world.

114

I had to go for myself and for my daughters even while they were elsewhere being children on that afternoon. This is what I want my daughters to know:
Don't be afraid.
Even of saying the wrong thing.
Only be afraid of what happens in a drought of love and imagination and a drought of one good friend and a drought of laughter. Be afraid of what happens when the wrong thing matters. Don't be afraid of ridicule. Don't be afraid not to be liked. Don't be afraid to be the only one or the first one. Be loud. Be unruly. Be who you are. Be connected to the world around you and strong original thoughts and learn to listen at times in true humility and remember joyful laughter. And let that connectedness and those thoughts and that humility and joyful laughter rule.

Sometimes the loneliness of your thoughts will visit on you an uncertainty and terror. Lorraine Hansbury wrote in "To Be Young, Gifted and Black":

> *Eventually it comes to you: the thing that makes you exceptional, if you are at all, is inevitably that which must also make you lonely...*

I only met Betty Shabazz once. In November, 1996.

I can't begin to imagine her loneliness. I can't imagine her pain. I can't conjure up her exhaustion or her amazing resources of will and compassionate intelligence. I can see her work. I can feel for her courage. I can listen for her daughters. And her grandchildren. And listen for what is to be done and not ignore it: the call for human arms for a family that was made in the great church on the day of remembrance. I can only hope to do any justice by a clarity of purpose and identity that can't be modeled or constructed or told but must be wholly authentic.
And by the promise to remember.

1997

Originally published in the East Hampton Star, June, 1997

Ruth's Skirts

And Ruth said,
Entreat me not to leave thee,
or to return from following after
for whither thou goest, I will go;
and where thou lodgest, I will lodge:
thy people shall be my people,
and thy God my God:
where thou diest, will I die,
and there will I be buried.

Ruth to Naomi from "The Book Of Ruth,"
The Old Testament, King James Version

I fold myself into scarves
of listening light
attempting to learn
that skill — listening —
my daughters will tell you
I have a long way to go!

they will tell you
much more than that
if you listen

       * * * *

The book of Ruth
was my favorite

Dad read me Ruth and Naomi
a regular bedtime request

Consonants of constance

I needed to taste the antique poetry
of loyalty
the stories of women
over and over
like butterscotch
or pancakes on Sunday

       * * * *

A young woman, Mbachi
came into our home

116

in summer
when sun lit bells on hammocks, noise and vegetables
from this earth made fertile
with a sculptor's hands and heaven's help

when we opened
old enough to know and give thanks
sank into night air
in love with every young voice
bellybutton pierce
daily salt wave plunge
each dusk and blue night
after months-long blood, a war we couldn't touch,
life sighed in us warm,
Neruda's odes, Amazonian strings
rocked us gently

some met
this young woman from Zambia
who smiled oceans
out loud
carried canoes in her heart
her eyes inheritance
of ink
they saw
my sister Safiya
in her face

* * * *

My sister sent you
I told her

* * * *

Choosing a skirt
to read for Palestine
the young woman told me:

wear this one
I see my mother in it
I see African women

Black
folds and waves
a skirt of rivers and stories
fabric for hands to hide
and children to dance

I wore it
What is your mother's name

Ruth.
Her name is Ruth.

I wore the skirt
of poems
skirt of prayers
skirt of a woman's life

listened in Washington D.C.
to a mother
her Rachel plowed down
by a tank called Caterpillar
in the land of Ruth
putting her Northwestern twenty three years
in the way of the Caterpillar
as it moved
slow and big and undeterred
towards someone's home
where am I in this mother's story
this poem I've written and re-written over time
which language today
puts its lips around this
cup of black skirts
and lost children)

> *Did they see her face*
> *Did they know his name*
> *Touch the color of her eyes with charcoal blindness*
> *Did they taste the names like water*
> *each name root a bullet*
> *Diallo, Baez, Washinawatok, Corrie, Ahmed...*

> * * * *

Dear Mother
of stolen children
in unlit corners

let us sew our skins together
a pouch of remembering

let me hold your eyes

like a flower

like a flame

let us be mother
together

we'll call it
        freedom!
taste olive
lick Cedar of Lebanon
wherever it grows

            * * * *

I wrap myself in my skirt
close my eyes
taste stone blood, a touch on the tongue
cold as child's medicine
hoping poems will come
like salve
a lu-shih from China
survived in the mouth of a Vietnamese girl
given to me
by my daughter
by her aunt, a poet
this is how we do it
each Ruth, each Naomi

            * * * *

In this gathering
a few old men
jackets still dusted
from traveling the oldest cities
seeds of figs

see their words
like skins
in a territory
stand up in the auditorium
when the numbers *Nineteen Sixty-Seven* are called out
flecks of Arabic fall in the air

* * * *

Ruth
speaks to me
from Zambia
all 73 dialects

She has no medicine

the fabric of her skirts
so plentiful

it could sift rice
it could hold tears
that dry into sheets

a skirt named home
a skirt called cousin
viral skirt
so black it survives

    * * * *

    Dear Safiya:

    I dreamt we took chemo
    together
    side by side
    in those awful chairs
    held out our arms
    watched the liquid
    move towards our veins
    pulled life stories
    from nurses
    made poems
    through i.v. inventions

    * * * *

I read the poems
of Naomi Shihab Nye.
Arabic heart
in American words
Texas
no easy place for olive, grandmother, home.

This word
appears

120

and I wonder
for whom translation might be needed:
: *Peace*

* * * *

Remember when we learned olive
might keep out cancer
poured rich oil over toast
and pasta
in sunshine
after Taxol

* * * *

P.S.

the apple tree we planted
for you

is yielding

small hard apples
I'm afraid to eat
Your grandson exclaims:
They are Grandma! Grandma!

the stone
at the foot of the tree
carries your name

stones of Chile
stones of Ireland

stones of memory
only poems live in

Your daughter is fine
Do you hear me
She is fine

* * * *

A poet close to us
said once:

Disease is an unfilled longing.

＊ ＊ ＊ ＊

Dear Ruth
you and I were born
just days apart;
your daughter Mbachi
is safe with us.
Medicine's on the way
with love and faith
from another Ruth
another Naomi

＊ ＊ ＊ ＊

A poet close to me
said:

The poem we will write
about our lives
begins

Dear Mother

Amama
Amama

＊ ＊ ＊ ＊

Fall, 2003

*Lu Shih is a Chinese poetic form used by the feminist Vietnamese poet Ho Xuan
Hu'o'ng in the 1700's
* Taxol is a cancer treatment used in chemotherapy
* Rachel Corrie was a 23 year old U.S. activist killed by the Israeli military
when she attempted to bodily prevent the bulldozing of a Palestinian home
in the Occupied Territories, in a program led by the International Solidarity
Movement. Caterpillar is the name of the bulldozer that killed her and that
is used to destroy the homes of Palestinian families in the Occupied Territories
* 1967 was the year that began the Israeli Occupation of the West Bank and Gaza
* Israelis and Palestinians often call each other "cousin."

About the Author

Kathy Engel is a poet; a communications/strategic planning consultant; a producer for social justice, peace and human rights organizations. Since 1979, she has been engaged full-time in building social justice, human rights and peace organizations and campaigns. She is committed to breaking boundaries, and infusing the imagination and thinking of the artist and the intellectual into the strategic planning for grassroots, community, national and international media and organizing efforts.

In 1983, Kathy founded the women's human rights organization MADRE and was the executive director for five years. Before that she worked at the Academy of American Poets, New York Mobilization for Survival and was the executive director of the Fund For Open Information and Accountability. She co-founded Riptide Communications, a public relations consulting firm for progressive organizations, in 1989. She now works as an independent consultant and teacher, with an emphasis on supporting the efforts of young artists and activists.

In December 2001 she conceptualized, scripted and co-produced "Imagining Peace," a dramatic reading and performance sponsored by MADRE to benefit women and children in Afghanistan. In 2002 she was project consultant and co-conceiver of Stand With Sisters For Economic Dignity, a political theater and media project of the Center For Community Change

In 2004, she produced and hosted a web-based radio show called "Out of the Box: art, politics & fun," and wrote a regular column called "Voice For Change" for Nuestra Prensa, published by the Southampton Press. In May 2005 along with musician Tiye Giraud, for the Correctional Association of New York's Women in Prison Project she produced "Who I Will Be," a performance piece with five formerly incarcerated women based on their words. She and Giraud co-founded KickAss Artists, a multi racial, cross generational coming together of artists and advocacy groups working towards a new humanism. She is a co-founder of the Hayground School and East End Women in Black.

In June 2005, she helped initiate RePlant Haiti, a reforestation effort in Haiti, launched with a Carnegie Hall Concert during which she performed her poem "For Haiti (after the floods)" with original choreography by Carole Alexis.

From September to December 2005, she worked with the People's Hurricane Relief Fund & Oversight Committee, after traveling to Jackson, Miss. and New Orleans following Hurricane Katrina.

Banish the Tentative, a book of poems, was published in 1989. Her work is included in numerous magazines and journals and *Racing and E-racing Language,* an anthology focusing on race and language (Syracuse University Press). She has performed, offered workshops, and given talks throughout the country. With Kamal Boullata, she is co-editor of *We Begin Here: Poems for Palestine and Lebanon* (Interlink Books, Olive Branch Press, Spring 2007). Her poem "The Kitchen" accompanies an art series and book by German Perez.

An adjunct professor at New York University's Tisch School of the Arts/Art & Public Policy Program and NYU's Gallatin School of Individualized Study, 2006-2007, she has been a fellow at the Macdowell Colony and The Blue Mountain Center and has been invited, along with artist Valerie Maynard and poet Alexis De Veaux, to be a resident at the Gaea Foundation's Sea Change Cottage.